THE COLLECTED POEMS

OF

T. HARRI JONES

GW00656287

The Collected Poems of
T. Harri Jones

Edited and with an Introduction by
JULIAN CROFT and DON DALE-JONES

GOMER PRESS
1977

First Impression - May 1977
Second Impression - September 1987

ISBN 0 85088 412 8

*This volume is published with the
support of the Welsh Arts Council*

Printed by:
J. D. Lewis and Sons Ltd., Gomer Press, Llandysul, Dyfed, Wales

for
MADELEINE

ACKNOWLEDGEMENTS

Mrs. Madeleine Mitchell, the poet's widow, for access to unpublished poems ; Granada Publishing Ltd., for permission to include poems from *The Colour of Cockcrowing* (1966) ; Mr. J. O. Davies, Librarian, Trinity College, Carmarthen, for help in securing texts ; Mrs. Edna Dale-Jones, for help with the correction of proofs.

CONTENTS

A NOTE ON THE TEXT

We have reprinted the poems from the four published volumes, *The Enemy in the Heart* (1957), *Songs of a Mad Prince* (1960), *The Beast at the Door* (1963), and *The Colour of Cockcrowing* (1966), omitting, however, the "Versions from the Italian of Roberto Sanesi" published in *Songs of a Mad Prince*. "Three Songs of a Mad Prince—I" first appeared in *The Enemy in the Heart* as "One Song of a Mad Prince" ; we have printed the later version. All of the poems have been checked against the manuscript versions preserved in the 'black book' in which T. H. Jones wrote fair copies of those poems which he wished to retain. A few trifling textual emendations have been made as a result. The "Uncollected Poems" represent a selection from the many as yet unpublished poems preserved in the 'black book' and are printed chronologically, covering a period from June 1959 to November 1964.

INTRODUCTION

Thomas Henry Jones was born at Cwm Crogau near Llan-afanfawr, Breconshire, on December 21st, 1921, the eldest son of Llywelyn Jones, also born at Cwm Crogau, and Ruth Teideman of Cardiff. His father's family had been associated with the Builth area for generations and his grandfather was well-known and respected in Llanafan parish. The family was poor : Llywelyn Jones worked as foreman roadman for most of his life and his father was a shepherd and rates collector. For the first ten years of his life Harri, as the family called him, lived in the isolated house at Cwm Crogau with little contact with other children. He was shy and liked to read and to walk by himself. Though his childhood was austere, he seems not to have missed material luxuries—"pen and ink he wanted", his father has drily observed. Unlike father and grandfather the boy did not speak Welsh. This seemed no disadvantage at the time, but the adult poet regretted his ignorance of his fathers' tongue. Those images of Wales which recur through the poetry are drawn from the Cwm Crogau landscape.

Harri was successful at Llanafan Primary School and became an avid reader. Prepared by his grandfather, he was very successful with recitations at local eisteddfodau. He began to write poetry.

In 1932 the family moved down to the valley road and settled at Trefelin, about three miles from Newbridge. Next year Harri entered the County School at Builth from which, with little effort, he won the County Exhibition to Aberystwyth in 1939. Contemporaries describe him as a scruffy but fiercely proud boy, passionately devoted to reading and writing poetry.

He went to Aberystwyth in 1939, but his studies were inter-rupted by service in the Navy from 1941 to 1946. By the end of what he called a boring war he had accumulated a large number of manuscript poems, useful apprentice-work of which little was ever to be published.

He took a First from Aberystwyth in 1947 and in 1949 gained his M.A. In 1951 he was offered a teaching appointment at the Portsmouth Naval Dockyard where he remained until 1959. From 1948 he was a regular contributor to *Life and Letters* both as poet and reviewer ; during the '50's *The Dublin Magazine* and *Dock Leaves* published his poems and short stories.

When it became clear that he was not to obtain an academic position in the U.K. he decided to emigrate to Australia. In 1959 he took up a post at the Newcastle college of the University of New South Wales where he taught English until his death in 1965. Soon the poet had a strong following in his adopted city ; his poetry readings became well-known and his poetry and reviews widely published in Australia.

By 1960 T. H. Jones had published two volumes of verse with Rupert Hart-Davis. *The Enemy in the Heart* (1957) had had favourable reviews ; *Songs of a Mad Prince* (1960) received lukewarm notice though it was recognized that the poet had considerable skill in his craft.

1961 was a productive year and one in which the poet's style noticeably developed. He moved from the rather strained craftsmanship of the early work into a more relaxed and direct style. Many of the poems are formal compliments, but they have an energy missing from the second volume. Sadly, the vitality of 1961 faded and from 1962 to 1964 this outwardly successful man was beset by depression and despair. It was evident from his intemperance and from his poetry that Harri Jones was facing a serious personal crisis. But the quality of his work did not decline—in fact, though he wrote fewer poems his poetry gained greater maturity.

In 1963 a third collection, *The Beast at the Door*, was published by Hart-Davis. In the same year Oliver and Boyd published his study of Dylan Thomas and he was commissioned to write a book on Yeats. He did not finish this, for on the morning of January 30th his body was found floating in a rock-pool at the base of some cliffs not far from his home. His widow, Madeleine, and a friend collected and edited a posthumous volume, *The Colour of Cockcrowing* (1966).

The work of Harri Jones is ample and varied but his achievement has yet to be given due recognition. The first two volumes show a style increasingly rejected during the '50's and '60's, rather artificial, with echoes of Dylan Thomas and Auden. Early work such as ' Poem ' (p. 7) is full of the Dylan Thomas ' booming ', while ' Portrait ' (p. 30) and ' Love ' (p. 35) show the influence of styles of the '30's. Perhaps the poet took his craft over-seriously and in the process lost energy of feeling. If, however, the love poems seem particularly artificial, this is because he preferred the structured to the spontaneous compliment : a love poem was a gift of craft to the loved one as well as an expression of passion.

Robert Lowell and R. S. Thomas seem to have influenced the later work which, after 1960, becomes more intellectual and directly confessional. It seems that the poet purposely maintains in his work a confusion between sin and guilt. His twentieth century mind told him that guilt was the product of social training while his temperament and cultural background counselled that sin was inherited. His struggle with a rigidly Calvinistic inheritance is seen in ' Cotton Mather . . . ' (p. 193), written in late 1964. At the end of Mather's monologue on the meaning of the witch trials at Salem in 1692 he asks :

> Were these things here in Salem ? Did help come ?
> Is God's good wilderness now purified ?
> Or must we fear and go in constant sorrow
> That we are still afflicted, that tomorrow
> May bring back to Salem that delirium ?

However, he believed that even if we cannot escape the wrath and testing of the Lord, we can nevertheless participate in the vitality of the Creation.

In the last years of his life Harri Jones oscillated between deterministic pessimism and vitalistic optimism. He was reluctant to accept the theological traditions of his fathers, but he also found it impossible to throw them off and live in the guiltless hedonism of a sunny but vacant climate :

> And the way unto Salvation
>   Underneath the Southern Cross
> Is no harder than the pathways
>   Where his fathers found their loss.
>
> (' Taffy Was Transported ' p. 179)

Forced to live abroad, he began to mythologise his feelings of exile. The Wales of childhood became the Eden to which he could never return ; Welsh ancestors and their Old Testament God were the example of the old life and old truths from which he had fled. But Wales was not Fern Hill and Mari Lwyd merely, it was also the harsh toil of Iago Prytherch and the hypocrisy of Chapel. These two aspects conflict in the exile's mind as he asks himself the inevitable question ' Back? ' (p. 181).

As the poet became more embroiled in personal crisis he turned more to the defeats and humiliations of his nation. He was able to see in Catraeth, in Camlann, in Saunders Lewis's brave but futile gesture, the hopeless heroism that he required himself when confronted by insuperable personal difficulties. The one hope of his last years was to remain indestructible as those symbols of survival, Wales and the thorn :

> This is the prayer of the bitter mind
> In the bloody dark :
> May I be relentless in the wind
> As the thorn . . .
>
> (' Thorn ' p. 186)

Harri Jones was an idealist with firm roots in the real earth of his non-conformist origins. Though many of his poems seem posed and contrived, they were attempts to impose order on a chaotic world by evolving a vision which should unite ideal and real, a style that would control a too fluent and wordy rhetoric. The best poems show few signs of influences because they give clear insight into his mind. ' Cotton Mather . . .' (p. 193), ' Simply to Write ' (p. 164), ' Girl Reading John Donne ' (p. 219), ' The Colour of Cockcrowing ' (p. 224), ' The Welshman in Exile Speaks ' (p. 118), ' A Storm in Childhood ' (p. 191) exemplify strengths which would surely have developed. T. H. Jones found in the last five years of his life ' the one inevitable word . . . the natural rhythm ' of a powerful style to give utterance to his struggling. His poetry shows, in an incomplete way, the dilemmas faced by a man who, because of the collapse of faith and the alienation produced by war, can no longer make sense of identity or love. His experience of these difficulties which are common to most of mid-century Western Europe was peculiarly Anglo-Welsh, but the record of his striving for answers is universal.

Julian Croft
University of New England
Armidale
New South Wales

Don Dale-Jones
Trinity College
Carmarthen
South Wales

THE ENEMY IN THE HEART

1957

POEM FOR MADELEINE

An ocean or embrace away
The weeping of my love fulfils
The sensual vision and the prayer.
Lost in the clarity of day,
Bewildered in the hurt of air,
My words are rain her sorrow spills.

A century or kiss ago
The generations in her eyes
Answered my urgency of prayer.
Now with the words I do not know
The vision in the random air
Of absence casually dies.

O love upon the distant shore,
O love so absent from my nights,
O image of my ecstasies,
O love, grant pardon to me for
Estranging time, estranging seas,
And all refusal of delights.

And grant me pardon, love, for pride
Expert in disobedience.
Forgive me that I could not reach
You when your longing cried.
And grant me pardon, love, for each
Failure of will, deceit of sense.

ANCESTRAL

Where we were born, a windy place,
A broken landscape of regrets,
High curlews calling, the careful men
Nursed their rocky memories in silence,
Avoiding the fat plains and their brute inhabitants.

Sullen or silver, the quick waters strained
Away from the bare ridges,
Seeking the fertile lands, the distant sea.
But the quiet men, the burdened women,
Aloof as foxes, clung to the ferned hillsides,
The stubborn memory, the confidence of God.

IN MY RETURNING

In my returning, the proud, flowered walking
Again in the loved, remembered land,
The valleys and hills of fact and legend,
Dear hospital and home of hopes and the sweet light,
I hear my heart a hedge of singing-birds,
And fill my eyes with the welcome of the hills ;
Walking with pride of race and singing craft
I magnify mountains, and suck in the air
Wales wears with memoried grace ;
In the green cwms I am again at home.

This is the blossomed quaystone where I end
My tattered seasons where begun ;
The flowered and feathered landscape
No longer a fading map of unloving strategy,
But a weight and a wonder of words
Not to be silently borne on my tender tongue ;
A pride and humility in my home-returning
To the dear and dark hills of legend
And fact that must be unleashed
In triumphant chorus to the bird-thronged air.

So to the dear land back I sing my own
Welcome, and in my tumbling pride
Hear it re-echoed by the rain-washed winds.
Wales wears an air, a grace, as a loved face
Motions to kisses on the letters of exile ;
And the intricate maps of farms
Welcome me back to a singing service,
A wonder of work, and the toil of love
In the green cathedrals of the sea-lapped,
Lovely, enduring landscape of fact and legend.

DIFFERENCE

Under God's violent unsleeping eye
My fathers laboured for three hundred years
On the same farm, in the expected legend.
Their hymns were anodynes against defeat,
But sin, the original and withering worm,
Was always with them, whether they excelled
In prayers, made songs on winter nights,
Or slobbered in temptation, women, drink.

I inherit their long arms and mountain face,
The withering worm sleeps too within my blood
But I know loneliness, unwatched by God.

AMENDS
(for Aneirin Talfan Davies)

There were no gods among that bitten grass,
Those rocky challenges, those wind-torn trees,
Only the presence of the ancient thunderer
Cloudy with terror of his images.

Buzzard and carrion-crow controlled the air,
The weasel slinked bloodthirsty through the woods ;
The fox and badger plundered and ran free
Where the grey winds made howling solitudes.

In that harsh landscape dreams were unconfined,
Dreams of hot sunlight and of older gods.
The coloured birds were singing in my head
When I set out to find the city roads.

Years after, in a thronged and barren parish,
I make old pictures of blackthorn and of pine,
The weasel and the crow, the mountain wastes,
And recall the only god that was ever mine.

POEM

Back to the loved sky and the humped hills,
The night-infested woods, the fish-cold brooks,
Pride of the fox and buzzard, all lonely terror
Of empty winds over Wales.
My fronded boyhood breaking like a tide
Flung up all contraries, the five gay kingdoms
Of sense, and, dominant as a cloud,
The obsolete map of chapels.
God, a crabbed shepherd on a misty path,
Whistled a thunderclap of truth.

The stammer of spring, the shout of summer
Drowned my husked prayers in the colours
Of time, and the jet of birth, the pain of growing,
The accident of death.
And rascal girls in the spilled calm of winter
In pews as warm as bed dreamed me to marriage.
Under a grassblade on the hill's lean rib
I found the bastard grief.
Bellmusic in the caverns of my sleep
Hymned my dark hope.

Orphaned by indolence and dreams,
Bridehaunted in that scriptural enchantment,
Lonely as priest or fox, I mouthed the seasons
And mourned undying time.
Lost in the quick and tangle of the groin
The dance and horror grew ; the spit of God
Cracked the wild globe, his dirty tears
Made sea and slime.
I found the hangman's tree, the livid prayer,
The hot mercy of fear.

7

Sighed breath and seed in the ominous weathers
Sprouted in glory ; in my green ruins
I sang like the rain ; and the cold dogs
Of my fathers ran
Howling in the graveyard of my heart.
The careless charity of time
Nailed me with silver to the four, crossed hills ;
A maggot murdered Eden.
Bird-droppings on the secret withered grass
Signalled where comfort was.

Rising like flower or the pressing bone
I broke and bloodied the holy circle,
And ran to the far, complaining seas
With a cloud round my head.
Now it is a long cry and a hard voyage
To that inheritance, that lost revolt,
The bell and candle in the fathered dark
Showing the tree of the dead.
Alone like a priest or a fox on the stubborn hills
I recall a child in Wales.

THE BALLAD OF ME

The wideawake sky went on for ever and ever
Over my boyhood, the eternal trees
Denied the fear of death, the flowers in their seasons
Were all immortal, and the birds sang
As everlastingly as the grass enchanted.

Tall men, tall women, went walking like trees
On my blue horizons, and catkin children
Swung in adventurous breezes to the tunes
Behind the chapels and cowsheds, the tunes
Of ferns and grasses, of druidic trees.

Slinked animals in water and on hillsides,
Weasel and badger, dandy fox and otter,
Fish were responsive to water-urges,
And birds hung and swung on the unseen edges of wind,
—And I among them walking and dreaming.

Near away sounded the sea, the ancestral summons,
But here in the hot pulse of the summer,
And vivid against the powdered skies of winter
Went on and on the preacher's sounding voice,
The word, the beginning, God's tremendous breath.

Can the buzzard escape from its nature, do other
Than kill from the depths of the sky ?
Can the otter, sinuous, splashless, split
The murmur of water with no thought of death ?
Shall a mountain pony be tamed by man or by weather ?

Shall the voice of the preacher be silenced ?
The poet hang like a gamekeeper's plunder
Nailed on a foreign street and an alien tongue ?
The fox is still prancing the hillside, the hawk
Has always dominion of air.

The streets break on my feet and my heart,
But boyhood's immortal kingdom is still
In the words of the preacher, the weave
Of the otter, the pad of the badger, the slink
Of the fox, the circle and swoop of the buzzard.

Still and still immortal waters move
About me, that lovely sky goes on
To where all words are woven in one word,
The first, immortal breath, the living breath
Shadowed in trees and grass and poets' words.

GORSE IDYLL

Her hair was like the sunlit gorse,
　Her body like the gorse on fire,
And what we knew of souls we'd take
　To any fair for hire.

I took her to the golden gorse,
　We made a gold to-do.
No deacon sighed with such content
　As we, when we were through.

Deacons and gorse in any land
　Would be so far apart—
And all the lands I walk through now
　I have a double heart.

POEM DEDICATED TO THE MEMORY
OF DYLAN THOMAS

From gorse and cinder hills I Adamed out
To take to name to praise all things I breathe
Before I burn in other breath, before
The tall shout take me and the nameless
Name me luckily and the praised be praise
And name and breath and all the burning.

Unparadised I found the spinning world
A noise in nothing and before a fall
I turned unribbed on the world's turning
To tread a morning name on printless days
And follow where it led the burning voice.

All else was accident, what errors fell
Or joys upshot as I moved out of grace
And five green seasons named the world for me.
Grained in the deep earth, lapped in the long water
I had lain who now moved tenderly
Towards a box of love and one last name.

The world is spinning and the world is named,
Adam unribbed and waking to his dream,
Five senses rule the world, and five
Are lucky in the last and burning name.

MY DAUGHTER ASLEEP

Here is the feature and fashion knows not bruise
Nor strident mark. The venom of the years
In these young veins has not yet made carouse :
These bones are not yet strained, flesh trenched with cares

This childgrace is a benediction of the blood,
Promise and resurrection : sleeping it signs
The argosy and ark its fathers made :
Denies, rewards heaven's anguish and earth's pains.

Here is the blossom and the laboured print
Not tempest-daunted yet, not by the beat and whirl
Of winds and waters strifesodden, savourspent,
Dragoned by days and nights to weary hell.

O morning miracle, O pride of peace,
When you have grown to stature and to guilt,
Look in the dance and agony of your days
Upon your child and learn how love is spelt.

OUT OF WALES
(A Poem for my Daughter)

Remembering today the land from which
You come, the huddled nonconformist hills,
The short grass sweetening the mountain sheep,
The stubborn ponies proof against the weather,
A shepherd's hazel stick and favourite bitch,
(My best-loved image of remembered Wales)
I watch you in your curled exotic sleep,
Waywardly growing, already another stranger.

THE VOCABULARY OF PROMISE

Nostalgic sailors in a dream of gardens
Have known a holy and immediate urge
To build upon the boredom of the sea
The city of invulnerable glass,
As poets, landfast in their private kingdoms
Of pain and beauty, see the lovers walking
Eternally two by two down the enchantment
Of children's smiles, lost in the dark forest.

Each takes from the vocabulary of promise
The little words like *Love* or *Sesame*
He seems to need, or would believe he needs.
Each feels in the contraction of his muscles
The world condense into infinity.
Each sees, or thinks he sees, the wild horizons
Rising above the ordinary phenomena
Of grief, bad luck, missed chances, or old age.

And all the time the treachery of blood
Revokes the casual promise of the dream,
The wasting bones prepare their wilderness,
The breath is tainted with its own decay.

The children in the enchanted wood explode
Into monsters, the lovers' contortions
And grimaces reveal the fear of death,
The sailors on the boredom of the seas
Forget the lovely city and their dream
Of gardens, and the helpless poets remain
Landfast within their private kingdoms
Of despair and pain, in terror making
Visions of love and beauty, and destroying
The value of each unenduring word
In the demoded vocabulary of promise.

THE ENEMY IN THE HEART

In the heart alone is the last enemy
The fatal friend who in the dim cathedrals
Of the towered and toppling waves
Makes you an image of all lost remembered loves
And kills the corn with terror of the sea
Rapes the rich earth with his sea-green betrayals.
Cast out romantically that spent savour
That lurking enemy whose glaucous veins
Spoiled the rich promise of your spousal saviour
And drowned your green blades in his greener veins.
But when you come to that last house of bone
His are the last embraces you discover
Though you go to your narrow bed alone
In no fond convoy with a friend or lover
That is the last speck on the unfolding chart
The murderer the foul the vulture heart.

POEM

The sensual landscape in his mind
Flowered in sudden fury, made him blind
To everything but that cathartic pain
Loosening the bonds of order in his brain.
He found the animals behind his eyes
Could take that verdant kingdom by surprise.
And when the brutal ravishing was done
He rested easily, took solace from the sun.

FOR RACHEL

The moment has gone by
When I could have stared
Unwinking in your eye,
And with assurance dared
To love you till I die.

Whether it was a lie
Or not, no longer matters.
Only you and I
Will know in what deep waters
We threw our love to die.

And only you and I
Will ever have to dream
Whether a lover's lie
Might not have made it seem
More difficult to die.

A QUESTION

What I really meant was this—
In this mutual robbery,
Disguised by word and look and kiss,
Of our fond identity,
Did either for a moment break
The unformulated covenant,
Would the other ever grant,
Even for this love's own sake
The right, should lover feel the mood,
To shrink back into solitude ?

LOST LOVE

The old extravagance of love eludes us.
The furtive seasons mock our torn regrets.
Desire, harsh as sunlight upon rock,
Lays sinewy hands upon us where we wait
For some forgotten symbol to announce
That water has been found, the wilderness
Hides somewhere the well, the sheltering trees,
The promised country we would not take by force.

THE SHAPES OF PITY

The shapes of pity reluctantly displayed
In dreams of daylight or the vivid darkness
Convince like fables ; the anarchy of hope
Is mute memorial to the griefs we made
Immortal animals to pad across the night,
To nuzzle us with centuries of fear.
The coloured dreams dissolve ; the faded past
Is crystal in the memory of a tear.

Pity is neither kindness nor cruelty,
But only witness to a world of sins.
The immemorial wilderness is weeping
Always, a desolation that in pain begins
And never ends but in some idiot laughter.
Across the desert wing the hideous birds
Whose cry is the remembered childhood nightmare,
The sweating Adam stammering for words.

Mirrored, the shapes of pity only reveal
Our frightened selves, distortions of our dreams.
Marooned in that discoloured wilderness,
Distractedly looking for the healing streams,
We hear the terrible chatter of those birds.
Their shadows blotting out the vacant sky
Remind us of our heritage of debt
And doubt, and the inexorable need to die.

The shapes of pity like bubbles elude us.
The storied animals of our nursery
Stalk monster-wise across our withered landscape.
Doom is despair ; the dead not dead are we.

19

The skeleton sprawled across the desert rock
Is smiling in its empty staring eyes.
All metaphors are murder ; death is human,
The one true pity, the undeceiving surprise.

SONNET

No rich complexity of flower or woman
   Could tease him from the clichés of remorse
Or his cold pondering on the inhuman
   Zodiac where he'd run his course.

He had no dreams to sabotage his tower,
   (There was a dream at first, and then no other).
In the selfconscious circle of his power
   Despair was faithful to him like a brother.

And yet decrepitude as subtle as a thief
   Mocked him obscenely, and made him rage.
The grave refusal of passion became grief
   When the obstinate years made him aware of age.

Weeping he left the tower for the park
   To watch the lovers waiting for the dark.

THE NEED FOR PARDON

The bitter thoughts that flowered in the garden
Made him afraid and lonely ; he was tired
Of the patterned richness he had once admired,
And conscious now of the great need for pardon.

Spurning the florid landscapes of his pride,
He eased his stiffness over the dark fence,
Thinking to climb back into innocence
Or a country where wisdom had grown old and died.

His long exotic sojourn had made him daft
Perhaps ; or possibly he had nurtured his mind
Too long on the formalism of solitude.

Pardon was not to be had where the lovers laughed,
Nor where the music was comfort to the blind.
—He wept quietly, alone in the wood.

POEM

In the towns and centuries of youth,
A multitude of exiles, the long voyages,
The dream, the dream had carried away
His heart and the poem's origin.

Waking on foreign pillows, he saw
His deepsea bride sail in a mist of tears
Away, away, and wept to be alone.
The dream had carried his heart away.

Turning and turning in his restless dark,
Interpreting the roots of memory,
He made his shrill cry to the absent morning.
His fled bride did not interrupt his prayer.

After the exiles there was no returning.
Not till the mandrake poem break the silence
Should the departed bride be celebrated.
The dream had carried his heart away.

MEDITERRANEAN : WARTIME

Drinking in bars around the sunlit harbours
My randy ghosts, persistent as coral,
Are muted in a dream
Of sulky, reluctant seasons,
An innocent world, another time than this.

Their passionate questions are dimly answered
By forgotten girls in this perpetual summer.
Reading in classic albums,
Only the wine-reek bears
Time and the unregenerate dream away.

The patient erotic sea surrounds us always.
The tawny lands reject our wistfulness.
Sun's kiss and hammer
Press our memories
To dark corners, to elusive fields.

Neither heroic nor lucky we take our turn
In the corrupted patterns of the war.
The indifferent tides
Perhaps will heal or hurt
The already lost, the impatient drinkers.

I hold the middle sea in a glass of wine
And listen to the vowelled bawdiness
Hiding a world of longings.
Taut in the sunlight
I throw my dreams upon the public bar.

Mother and mistress the wine-dark enemy
Estranges us in time as well as space.
Persistent ghosts
In this perpetual summer
Dream of slow seasons in the sunlit harbours.

THE DEFINITIONS OF CIRCUMSTANCE

Removed from the definitions of circumstance,
This love might prove to be the pure
Involvement in the holy ambience
Our vision coincides with now no more.

For now harsh vistas of regret and pain
Intrude upon the unaccomplished eye ;
The gesture of our intricate design
Lacks something of conviction, suggests a day

Devoted to emotions not less brash
Than those that first conflicted in the hour
When the serpent, confident in the lush
Though innocent garden, demonstrated power

To make distinction between good and good,
And separated with enduring art
The mutual compassions of our blood,
Writing the book of knowledge with that hurt.

No legendary comfort from this rock
Releases you, for my abortive mission
Only proves conclusively I lack
The purity of that heroic passion

Which might have visited your sacrifice
Immaculately armed to kill the beast,
And, deft and courteous on the baffled seas,
Encounter you in no disguise of lust.

Thus, hampered and defined by circumstance,
The limitations of this love can prove
Only what we guessed before by chance :
We can expect no more from human love.

NOT MUCH COMFORT

No convert even now to gentleness,
The limbs like holly discomfort any bed,
And dribbled memories and stale desires
Make puddles in the mind—this consolation
Can still evoke approximate peace :
Vehemence of my dreams and my daft words
Gave me one woman's summer.

Now I would prefer a little fire.

STANZAS IN A MIRROR

Tomorrow round the corner,
The country through the mirror,
The man I may become,
These betray me daily,
These distract me wholly
From perfection of the dream.

Poems I am not writing,
Like love that may be waiting
For me to play my part,
Can give me grief and terror
Like any other error
Or self-inflicted hurt.

And staring in the mirror
At my own continued murder,
I see behind my eyes
The man I may become
Take posession of my dream
With his assured lies.

Tomorrow round the corner,
Says the liar in the mirror,
Will give you the command
Of art and love and living.
Dreaming is believing,
And easier in the end.

So daily in the mirror
I contemplate my murder
And listen to his lies.
Tomorrow round the corner
I may be older, wiser—
But when I die, he dies.

And when I die, the mirror,
Survivor of my murder
And witness of my dream,
Will it tell the coroner,
Tomorrow round the corner,
What I have become?

PORTRAIT

By foreign calculation led to infer
That the absurdities in the mirror were
The very lineaments of pride,
He forswore abstraction, bargained for a kiss.
And this was virtue in him, this
Kept many foul shadows at bay until he died.

Had he for any reason done otherwise,
Insisted on the mirror's fantastic lies,
The self-spun, self-informed design,
Who could have reached him from across the border
In the other country of disorder
Where the will is stubborn and even loves decline ?

But he made his choice, and this in him I praise :
However he remembered his mirror days,
He never allowed regret
To create more than a little fever in his blood.
He went about his work, ate solid food,
Got children. His memory has some fragrance yet.

MY ANGEL

An angel slept within my side
Lulled upon delirium's tide
Deaf to the voices of my power
Roaring to signify their hour
Blind to the gaudy caricatures
To which my eyes set signatures
Dumb to the knocking in my brain
That witnessed to an outer pain.
The angel slept within my side
Not knowing if I lived or died.
I hung my angel on a cross
To testify a bitter loss.

POET

Gartered with love and gadded with ambition,
Tethered to a suicidal stake,
Noting the way waves break, hearts break,
The trapped man, ruttish in condition,
At the cavorting choruses of bells and birds
Stretches between the envy of his ears
A twist and torrent and thunder of words,
—His blood is fearful only of his fears.

Harnessed in lust and whipped by hope,
Dreaming of roses in suburban sun,
But watching lissom movements as they run,
He has to hang himself in his own rope,
Though he'd prefer at home to read his paper,
Back or tickle his fancy, paint a wall,
Cheat or assist or disavow his neighbour,
—And hear nothing, nothing at all.

But the thud and splendour of the stallion feet
Splash and spurn the waves of his blood ;
He must find flowers erupting from the mud,
Measure and mortify his own heartbeat,
Poke and peer into every corner,
Put his burnt hand back in the fire.
—The worst is, he is already his own warner,
And dead already of his own desire.

CRITICAL ENCOUNTER

This critic was too subtle is my guess.
   I was dismayed at first, but later thought
His ambiguities concerned me less
   Than the cold comfort that my poem brought.

Not that I'd trust entirely my own wit
   To tell me what I mean by every word.
Doubtless he's right when he untangles it—
   But then I have a sense of the absurd.

Would it have made any difference
   If I'd disclaimed responsibility ?
No. For the critic must have confidence—
   The poet makes do with fallibility.

So we agreed at last to separate,
   And go our ways, and try to understand.
We did not make our gestures desperate—
   Just smiled, and shook each other by the hand.

And left. The poem still remains.
   Now that I read it in a different light,
(How cunningly I picked the fellow's brains !)
   I could so easily believe him right.

A PLEA AGAINST ARMISTICE

After the bickering among the trophies,
Our almost banal internecine wars,
The casual intrusion of the stars
On our blurred vision of hostilities
Reminds us, not without a certain sneer,
Of concepts once held honourably dear.

Advantage of that momentary pause
May not be taken easily—not, at least,
Without some soft placating of the beast
Who lays upon the neck his cloying paws
Of reason, justifying every act
By irresistible appeal to fact.

Better then to shut the image out
Of old ideals still decorating heaven.
The beast is at our back. That is the given
Riddle in the core of every shout
With which the last ambition of despair
Attempts to crack the agony of air.

Better sustain among the tarnished trophies
This subtle vanity of bickering
Than hear again those ruined voices sing
That beckoned childhood over famous seas.
Let us, beneath the indifferent charm of stars,
Acquit us in our lost, inferior wars.

LOVE

Beggars snuffle in doorways,
   Women offer their wares,
But I have seen the location
   Of hell upon the stairs.

Dogs howl in the moonlight,
   Stones cover the dead,
But I have heard the clamour
   Of devils in the bed.

Time coughs and threatens,
   Evil are the streets,
And love is murdered nightly
   Between the loving sheets.

DEBATE

My love and I held long debate
   With wild and cautious art.
The question moved was, Which could do
   The other greater hurt ?

Our double art was wasted
   In that attempt to prove
Our dialectic could be used
   To demonstrate our love.

Theorems end expectedly,
   And so with our debate.
Each of us was the loser,
   Each is alone tonight.

THE BRIDEGROOM

Impatient, debonair,
The bridegroom sits alone
In a sexy room
With his mirrored stare.

His unclenched love unfolds
A history of light
Which the improbable
Ceremony holds

Aloof from him. His eyes
Define a miracle
As, in the glass,
Identity dies.

And the room's ambience
Holds as a cunning vase
The nourished flower
That had been innocence.

STARE-IN-THE-FACE

Stare-in-the-face said to me,
'Do not be capable of doubt.
If in the mirror you should see
The captive beast, perplexity,
Be brave and let it out.'

Stare-in-the-face admonished me,
' Out in the open factual air
The niggling animal you see
Will vanish in its liberty
And leave you honest there.'

Stare-in-the-face was kind to me,
He meant each word he said.
He did not know that liberty
Disposes not of doubt, but me.
He does not know I'm dead.

INTIMATIONS OF MORTALITY

There on that hot, unlucky bed,
  (Miles away, miles away)
Embarrassed but intrepid still
The boy who would be admiral
Went down beneath the ninth wave,
Hearing the laughter in the love—
  You are unlucky, no one wins today.

Drained and warm upon that bed,
  (Miles away, miles away)
Brave in recovery from his fever
The would-be lone explorer
Died in the tangles of the trees
Hearing the parrot mockeries—
  You are unlucky, no one wins today.

Emptied on that unlucky bed,
  (Miles away, miles away)
The boy who'd be a jaunty gambler
Careless what his fates uncover,
Died at the flicking of a card
To call a bluff he had not heard—
  You are unlucky, no one wins today.

Wordless on that unlucky bed,
  (Miles away, miles away)
The beardless poet proves his love
Who now will fill his paper grave
With words he heard before his fall,
The words the winner says to all—
  You are unlucky, no one wins today.

TWO

Deadlocked and still indubitably two
This loyal pair now struggle to undo
The grapple each laid on the other's body
To obtain and hold impossible unity.

Each in the struggle lacks desired scope
For the bold acts commensurate with hope
That could effect the needed dissidence
And sanction each in his own difference.

Tangled among the loving and the lies
Each in the mirrors of the other's eyes
Reads the reluctance of his own admission
That nothing now can alter his condition.

Helplessly the struggle still goes on
Although each knows no victory can be won,
For each is nourished by the other's body,
Lockfast and lonely in duality.

And every twitch and writhe draws tighter yet
The scarifying and necessary net
That once promised impossible unity
To separateness of body and body.

PROBLEMS OF LANGUAGE :
OLD MAN, YOUNG GIRL

Language is always dogma, said the sage,
Who had not heard
Your one derisive word
Topple the tower of my presumptuous age.

The ruins of dead languages reveal,
The poet said,
Always that love is dead.
He had not seen the life my shards conceal.

I cannot find in poet or in sage,
In them or you,
Anything now to do
Except to put delusion in a cage

Of other words, and hope again that rhyme
Will deaden grief.
—But can I cheat belief,
Who failed so obviously at cheating time ?

SITUATION

Your eyes are telling the weather back
 In a summer still as stone.
Under the hot and innocent skies
 A backward wind has blown
 My love to be alone.

This was not told upon the chart
 You gave me for my own
To guide me to a green, green place
 My love had always known
 Was yours and mine alone.

Now I am withered in this wind
 Of summer like a stone.
Your eyes, the chart, the innocent weather
 Leave me here alone,
 In a green place alone.

HOMAGE TO WALLACE STEVENS

I

The crude constructions of fortuitous dream
Flare by, but in his coloured room
A clown lays on his colours in a rage.

It is a rage that pedantry or suave
Analysis cannot dissuade or touch.
It is a rage for colours as they are.

And colours as they are are tricksy things.
The clown is helped to find them as they are
By music he evokes from a guitar.

Suppose the colours of the original sea,
The sea of syllables at first and last,
Primal oh-ho and last ironic ha :

The clown, then, as he rides, rides on that sea.
The clown, then, as he sings, sings with that sea.
He matches the sea's rage with his rage.

II

Displacement of our dreams cannot provide
Per se for symbols of reality.
We have to recognize before we learn.

It is a tedious process for the weak.
The sure music that the clown evokes
Can help us as he lays his colours on.

It is the colour of ourselves we seek.
But how are we to know it when we see
Unless some angel plucks the plangent strings,

Unless the raging sea resolves itself
To order as the raging clown commands,
Like the responsive blue of his guitar ?

The clown makes music of the raging sea,
Finding the ultimate of colour there
Which was before he spoke or lifted hand.

III

No other angel interposing here
With formula or ban can disappoint
Those who have listened to the blue guitar.

Rage, clown, among the colours of your room
And memories of the necessary sea,
Blue music of your ultimate guitar.

We have discarded other colourists,
And hope in time we can discard ourselves
Into the ordered raging of the sea.

Then we shall know the colour of ourselves.
Meanwhile we too are more or less aware
That colours in themselves are tricksy things.

We listen to the raging of the sea,
And to the raging of the clown who plucks
Blue secrets from his blue and plangent strings.

MERLIN'S LAMENT

I knew those rigid kings
   In their erected state,
And knew their supine queens,
   Their lying fate.

I gave their nightmares names,
   Answered their riddles ;
Told them what the signs meant
   On graves and cradles.

I told them how to hunt
   The incredible animals
And return victorious
   With the true symbols.

But for all my knowledge
   The table cracked and broke ;
Died all the young gallantry
   In the battle smoke.

I'm left alone in my wisdom
   With a barren love,
The ruined land around me,
   The birdless sky above.

IV. SONGS

SONG FOR A TIME OF TROUBLE

When the lion brings to the broken city
The dialectic of hate
When the bird screams across the heavens
Its anger and grace
Show your sulky hearts on your sleeves
Believe that grief is beautiful.

When you see beyond the ruined waters
Tall images of towers
Or when you quiver in the mountain grass
Like hares in their forms
Hide your vivid hearts in your hands
Understand grief is terrible.

SONG

Ten weathers at my finger-tips
May make me wise
When the lost kingdoms of my eyes
Are branch and blossom on my lips.

A cloud and thunder on my brow
May make me sad
When the rough blood turns dark and bad
To stop the singing on the bough.

A rising sun within my heart
May wither me,
Drying the sap, burning the tree,
And killing all my country art.

O weathers, thunder, golden sun,
Make me sad and numb,
And all my singing branches dumb,
To see my stolen countries gone.

SONG

O who unribbed me where I lay
Sleeping like Adam that bright day ?

The dancing light, the dancing blood,
Those images of clangorous love,
What were they to the death of pride
And what ambitious verse had said ?

Rage and compassion I had known,
And the harsh smouldering to possess
Some intimacy deeper than
The touch of wavebright bone on bone—

But who unribbed me where I lay
Sleeping like Adam that bright day ?

SONG

There is a country of disorder
Far away, near to us
Where tatters of our lives provoke
Neither homily nor joke,
And our spindrift dreams assume
Proportions of an ampler doom.
Every action is a kiss.

There is a country of disorder
Far away, near to us
Where sandy moments do not bite
Gradually at our delight,
And the erosion of the sea
Is only song continually.
Every action is a kiss.

There is a country of disorder
Far away, near to us.
Where is your passport ? Where is mine ?
Patrols of fear and chance decline
Although we have declared our sins
To show us where that land begins.
Every action is a kiss.

SONG

Interlocked upon the bed
The lovers do what they must do,
But when it's done, they lie apart,
Knowing in the separate heart
That one is one and two is two,
Number is for ever so.

Sprawled upon the glittering plain
The armies at the end of day
Know that even the salty fight
Cannot their separates unite
In that long roar of interplay.
Number is for ever so.

Whatever words have sought to tell,
Lovers and armies sought to do,
Neither the one nor other fight
Can these poor separates unite,
For one is one and two is two,
Number is for ever so.

SONG OF THE DANDY BONES
(*for Ted*)

It was not in the lubber lands
Nor in the city made with hands
The windy weather made me go.
It was not anywhere *you* know,
Sang the dandy bones as they swung in the tides.

It was not woman's kindling heat
That made my roaring pulses beat
Or any trick that *you* may know,
Impelled me on my way to go,
Sang the dandy bones as they swung in the tides.

But wilder wishes made me ride
The mocking horses of the tide
And in the windy weather find
The peace unknown to lubber mind,
Sang the dandy bones as they swung in the tides.

Let lubber bones in graves forget
The windy weather rocks me yet,
But I am scavenged clean and free
To feed the harvest of the sea,
Sang the dandy bones as they swung in the tides.

THE PRIDE OF THE MORNING

As I walked out in the pride of the morning,
  Too young to admire and too old to deride,
I saw the whole city was bonny with fire
  And everyone else had suddenly died.

So I walked for a while in the pride of the morning,
  Alone, with a strut, and a dandified smile,
The king of the fire, the lord of the city,
  Flamboyant, alone, and proud for a while.

But alas for the dandy, alas for the king,
  Alas for the pride that is nourished on fire,
The flames as I passed them were courteous with homage,
  But my heart wanted someone to see and admire.

My heart shrivelled up in the pride of the morning,
  Played traitor, alas, to the dandy and king,
Because I was walking alone in my splendour
  And the fire was deaf to the song I could sing.

A NEW SONG OF OLD DESPAIR

The ballad's wormy eye
Glitters with hunger,
All history's malice
Shrivelled to metaphor.
Where is the lee of the gallows ?
Asks the old sailor.

The sermon's bony shout
Is not of pardon,
Being too much aware
Of necessary sin.
Where is the lee of the gallows ?
Asks the old sailor.

Bloodspattered tragedy
Pays no debt off,
No more than comedy's
Racking laugh.
Where is the lee of the gallows ?
Asks the old sailor.

Nothing written or said
Dodges paradox.
There is shelter to be found
In the lee of all rocks.
Where is the lee of the gallows ?
Asks the old sailor.

A SONG OF THE DAYS

On Monday it is the waking
Drenched in the light
And the cast dream.
On Monday it is beginning.

On Tuesday it is the drumming
Dazzle of words
And the hurt tongue.
On Tuesday it is the saying.

On Wednesday it is the bruising
Delight of hands,
The calloused fingers.
On Wednesday it is the touching.

On Thursday it is the rushing
Together of all
Sweet, sour savours.
On Thursday it is the tasting.

On Friday it is the burning
Of weed and incense,
Confusion of air.
On Friday it is the smelling.

On Saturday it is the bringing
Of five truants
Together. The five
On Saturday are ending.

On Sunday it is the praying
With the five and more.
Tomorrow is Monday.
On Sunday it is everything.

DEDICATORY POEM

These disturbances now I dedicate
To you, the proud disturber
Of more than blood, deceiver
Of more than sense. No surrogate
Could ever satisfy
Lover or poet for his exquisite lie.

I do not ask you to remain content
With riddling ambiguities
To resolutions that may please
Your vanity or flatter my intent ;
But ask you to believe
Poets and lovers are fated to deceive.

If there is any comfort for grey hairs
In proudly saying, *Look,*
A poet yesterday put in a book
His love for me, its triumphs and despairs—
That comfort's yours.
Do we regret love dies, while art endures ?

Disturber, take with no reluctant hand
This offering ; look with no cold eye
On each affectionate lie.
Only the certainty you understand
Gets you the gift. Be wise,
And listen to no other poet's lies.

A WISH FOR MY ELDEST DAUGHTER

Let her remember in outrageous youth,
Let her remember in every dreaming bed,
The women poets praise are mostly dead,
Though some of them had stumbled on this truth,
That love is only a gift to loving eyes,
Before they listened to those rhythmic lies.

Let her not know extravagant despair
Because no poet finds her wholly fair.

SUNDAY ON THE BEACH
(*for Rhiannon*)

The wind was clouting the beach
With proper motherly slaps
That did not hurt perhaps
Though it seemed they were meant to teach
Something how to behave
In the presence of wind and wave.

Among the knots of knees,
By right assuming ease
In the water's salt and blue,
A baby laughed and ran,
A blob with legs and arms,
A blonde hullabaloo,
Squealing for liberty,
To jump in inches of sea
And lie in the sucks and laps
Of the little waves.

Watching her nakedness
And bellylove of the water,
Though I know the harms of the sea,
Though I know the harms of the crowd
In their best brown Sunday suits
And their candy frocks, though I know
That, however unique, my daughter
Will behave as the crowd behaves
In certain essential pursuits—
Though I know all this, I dare
To make for her one prayer :

Though she may not escape
That last and lurking shape
By the transfigured sea,
May she assume a rage
Decrepitude or age
Or mere external stain
Are powerless to touch.
Let her, like the sea,
All her life retain
Grace of body and mind
No accident can smutch.
As even the winter bough
Recalls its glory of leaf,
Let her, in spite of grief,
Stay beautiful as now.

SONGS OF A MAD PRINCE

1960

ECLOGUE

At wedding-feast or country fair
No seasonal metaphors disturb
   The nonconformist ghost.
Remote as myth, he hovers where
Ancestors, foaming on the curb,
   Are ridden by the lost.

And easy in his craft he prays
Purgation of such vanities.
   The guests endure and smile.
Though he denies their holidays,
The sailors on the broken seas
   Laugh at his sullen tale.

The unregenerate at feast
Or fair or straddled on the seas
   Are dabbled in the blood ;
But he, his victim and his priest,
Is swaddled in such fantasies
   Of evil and of good

As turn about his sorry heart
In formal, convoluted prayers
   For those who, smiling, lost,
Ignore his preordaining art
To damn them at their feasts and fairs
   And make them pay the cost

For sins too readily forgiven
By easier churches, milder gods.
   That unrelenting ghost
Is tenant of a narrow heaven,
And checks with terror of his rods
   The future in the past.

MARTYRDOM

This is authentic dark. Startling the air
Comes the beat, beat of the heart : the breath
Shivers unseen. *Is there anything there* ?
How can we image the lonely moment of death ?

Then suddenly all breaks, dissolves to light,
Such light as childhood only had adored.
Calm, he receives in the transfigured night,
Burning, the undesired arrows of the Lord.

DEATHBED

In the room of the curse and the web of prayer,
The room of the conversations in the dying head,
The flowers unfold and expand under the eyelid
Like confessions. A stained envelope of fear
Contains the little innocence and guilt
Which now become enormous and explosive.

Stifled faraway sounds only serve to enhance
The silence of his breathing. Time's erosion
Has suddenly stopped. He is back at the dark confusion
Where he bloodily broke on the world in a startled entrance.
Now we must parcel out his innocence and guilt
Among ourselves, but cannot make it any less explosive.

REFLECTIONS ON TRAGEDY

The meaning of fear is not apparent
In the trapped smile ;
The shriek and penetration of the truth
Evoke, perhaps, only a casual response
From the audience locked in its own distance.

Emblems and similitudes of fear
We know only
In the remembered lines and situations.
It is easy to identify with the pathos of the hero
The reconstruction of a private sorrow.

And with some tart reflections on despair
To imagine glibly
Incredible landscapes moulded by catharsis
To a resemblance of the needed city,
Free of the tax of guilt, restriction of pity.

It is better, then, to encounter the dilemma
In the stretched night
Alone, and not to expect the answer
To be as simple for us as the grief of Lear,
Or Hamlet borne off in the applauding air.

True tragedy may touch us, yes. What counts
Is the willingness
To recognize in the soul's desert
The one flower that holds the real meaning of fear
And to nourish it in every admonishing air.

A SONG FOR YOU AND ME

Who would want to pardon
The sunlight for infringing
The protocol of night,
Or disinfect the garden
Of the lithe, estranging
Serpent of delight ?

Dispersal of our roses
On random, interloping
Breezes of despair
May, one half-supposes,
End our banal hoping
In the vanity of air.

After breeze and flower
We still may see remaining
The toughness of the briar ;
Nor is it in our power
To meditate disdaining
The serpent of desire.

So we abjure pardon,
And concentrate on winning
From every chance and mood
The cherished secret garden
Where the serpent in his sinning
Knows not solitude.

FOUR

Four corners of the narrow room I'm in
Betray possession of the face and gender
Of each disputed context of surrender
To the archaic images of sin.

Four images, each armed with blast and flame,
Contract the narrow story of this room
To slavering minutiae of doom
After a shoddy mimicry of fame.

Four murders, crouching with possessive haste,
Leer at the mirage of my fortitude,
Waiting to occupy the solitude
That was my heart before love laid it waste.

Four beasts will spring at me eventually
From dusty lairs in corners of the room
To tear me in the processes of doom
Already studied in love's nursery.

THE FORMULAS

Distinguished and remote, the formulas arranged
Their uninvited discipline about the room
With all the deliberate neat gravity of doom
As if their mere portentousness of advent changed
Our inheritance of flurry and our neurotic fuss
To dignity of proper ends somehow exalting us.

This had not been expected ; though the accusation
Frigidly made by the mirror's candour had earlier warned
That our love of freedom might more easily be suborned
Externally than by our timid hesitation
To refuse the careful propaganda of despair
That followed us each night up every guilty stair.

So now in the ultimate impotent disgrace
Our humble mouths and knees make at last the correct prayer,
While the formulas display their clever menacing flair
For rejoicing cynically at our loss of hope and face ;
And all the hostility of their discipline
Contrives to make us repent of an unreal sin.

ADDRESS TO MY FACE

My double darling , witty dismay
Of every mirror, morning disaster
To the equilibrist, Hope,
And hangover of every day,
Must you indefinitely stay ?

Old obsession, favourite dream
Of my romantic ghost (stalking
Tiger among the flower ladies),
Are you, my discredited theme,
Ugly as you begin to seem ?

Constant companion, friend or foe,
Inevitably you disguise
Somebody I might have been,
Though nobody can ever know
Whether or not it's better so.

I shrug my shoulders in the glass
And end the diatribe.
You cannot answer anyway,
And so we let the matter pass,
—Until I meet you in another glass.

BALLAD

As I was going by the sweet legend
  (Believing in roses and crossing my fingers)
A sudden woman waylaid and wed me
  (O withered the roses, my fingers are stiff).

Where are you going in the sweet legend
  (Believing in roses and crossing your fingers)
As if you don't know that all legends are doomed
  (The roses will wither, your fingers grow stiff)?

I am just going in the sweet legend
  (Believing in roses and crossing my fingers)
Because I am young and not yet done dreaming
  (O withered the roses, my fingers are stiff).

Better for you in the sweet legend
  (Believing in roses and crossing your fingers)
To linger with love while yet there is time
  (The roses will wither, your fingers grow stiff).

Who will direct me in the sweet legend
  (Believing in roses and crossing my fingers)
To find my true love or to dodge my true doom
  (O withered the roses, my fingers are stiff)?

I will direct you in the sweet legend
  (Believing in roses and crossing your fingers)
I'll be your true love, your darling, your doom
  (The roses will wither, your fingers grow stiff).

Then I'll stay with you in the sweet legend
    (Believing in roses and crossing my fingers)
Forgetting the end of all dreaming is doom
    (O withered the roses, my fingers are stiff).

I lingered and rotted in the sweet legend
    (Believing in roses and crossing my fingers)
With the woman who loved me and left me my doom
    (O withered the roses, my fingers are stiff).

Still I am singing of the sweet legend
    (Believing in roses and crossing my fingers)
Long, long ago my dreaming was over
    (O withered the roses, my fingers are stiff).

LOVE POEM

The imperception of your absences
Defines remoteness that exists
After denial and the tousled lists—
You still can keep important distances.

Matter it were indeed for a great wonder
If you had not that gift of going off.
Would it not make even the pious scoff
If what we'd joined we could not also sunder ?

In love, it seems, our greatest need is this :
To let the other go, alone, apart
Into the farthest regions of the heart
Without the least disturbance of a kiss.

A LESSON IN GRAMMAR

I never learned to say it properly,
To join two pronouns with an active verb,
—That's how I see it now with the acerb
Grammarian's somewhat faded faculty
For conjugation and analysis—
To say, I love you, with due emphasis.

For in my lesson-days I always found
This grammar much less needful than the rest
And never really put it to the test,
But tucked it in a footnote as unsound
And doubtful, lacking in authority
Except by hearsay and empirically.

Now, of course, I find it difficult
To say the sentence never properly learned
In youth when tongues may easily be turned
And twisted to obtain a glib result.
But pondering my lesson-book today,
I fear it will be harder to unsay.

ADAM

Walking alone in the garden of day
In the virgin weather,
Did he dream that sweat of intercourse
Or thought might stain and strain
His bright prophetic body ?
Or that God's wrath would cloud
Over their agony together
And rob them of their innocent sleep ?
That he and she
And all the unsullied skies would weep ?

A LATE QUARREL

All other quarrels being now forgotten,
When love that knew not time discovers age,
It is good we feed the remnant of our rage
Upon these trivialities. Love's rotten,
Maybe, but these flickerings of strife
Show that it still retains a little life.

VOYAGES

In the mornings where my mercies were
   The ballad in my breast
Hurt like a cough ; ambition ripped
   Like tidal ice
Across my voyages, my green unrest.

Authentic violence compelled
   Those random voyages.
Love's big and blizzard clutch
   Could daunt my song
To silence in the uproar of the seas.

Sometimes a lucky island held
   My obstinate desire
And let the daunted song erupt
   Out of its ache
And die in the exhaustion of its fire.

But always other landfalls promised :
   The ballad in my breast
Persisted in its hurt, and drove
   My green pursuit
Over the endless waters of unrest.

THE LAST REGRET

If you should come, a slack-loined ghost,
To trouble corners of my sleep
I shall remember that the most
Demanding lust, being dead,
Can do no more than creep
And ask for comfort in my bed.

And I shall press dried breasts and say,
What have I now for your delight?
Down on your bony knees and pray,
Old man, forgiveness of your sins.
Then, shrinking in the night,
Learn how the last regret begins.

VILLANELLE

Something there is not cured with a kiss.
To be distracted to a greater rage—
The need of the heart was never less than this.

It is a cry not apt for emphasis
Or slick manipulation on a page.
Something there is not cured with a kiss.

Nor is it cured when you hear the hiss
The expiring serpent makes in his old age.
The need of the heart was never less than this.

It is a cry you cannot hope to miss
Sometime on your ragged pilgrimage.
Something there is not cured with a kiss.

Nor is it cured when paralysis
Subtly invades your make-do equipage.
The need of the heart was never less than this.

And at the end of all experiences
We are distracted to a greater rage.
Something there is not cured with a kiss.
The need of the heart was never less than this.

WORKERS OF THE WORLD, UNITE
(*for Stanley*)

On the worn and public grass
Underneath the bourgeois sky
Proletarian lovers lie
Careless of the crowds that pass
And cast an eye.

In the perfect, workers' state
They shall lie on beds of down
And their likings consummate
Unexposed to public frown
And torch shone down.

Or should any lovers sigh
For a bit of love on grass,
The State will always let them lie
Underneath the workers' sky
If they've a pass.

Proletarian lovers know
In their own desired park
Only the keepers come and go
In a routine to-and-fro
After dark.

For the State must still ensure
Even in such lusts divine
That rutting comrades still make sure
That their passions keep the pure
Party line.

And that on the careless grass
They still remember that coition
Even with a government pass
Is not just fun for lad and lass—
It means fruition.

So the servants of the State
Severely look by night and day
That the lovers consummate
Their joys to benefit the State,
Not merely play.

But underneathe the bourgeois sky
Where heartless crowds may pass,
The unenfranchised lovers lie
Exposed to every sneering eye
On the bourgeois grass.

NURSERY RHYME

Eve's first laughter shook the leaves
When that serpentine clown
Taught her the merriest words he knew,
All fall down.

When Adam failed to see the joke,
She smoothed away his frown
By whispering into his ear,
All fall down.

When Cain and Abel drove her mad,
Clutching at her gown,
She showed them the merriest game,
All fall down.

And you, my dear, had better learn
This game of great renown.
Be good, my dear, be careful, for—
All fall down.

INVOCATION

Lady, the stilted bird who gave me love
Has vanished, and the land
Is suddenly forlorn. Between bare trees
I can see nothing but the nothing
That is sky, and the withered bed
Where once the bird drank freely.
O lady, will you send again the beat
Of wings, the drumming clangour,
The bird, and water for its sustenance
To this dry land ?
Or must I watch the trees now slowly dying ?

LONG-AGO LOVE

My long-ago love goes lightly through the summer
As random as a dream, and the ruined boys
Forget their debt to time to see her smiling.
But I, marooned in winter, remember.

My long-ago love speaks in the old language
To listeners drowsy in her summer heat,
Forgetful of the turn, return of seasons.
But I, marooned in winter, remember.

O young men glad to see my long-ago love,
Do not remember in the smile of summer
That winter comes and the ruin of your joys.
Let me, marooned in winter, remember.

Let me, in memory of my long-ago love
Make one more dream of how she looked in summer,
And how I smiled in response to her smiling.
Let me, marooned in winter, remember.

LADY IN A GARDEN

Penned in the garden of her own disaster
The lady feels the cold creep to her knees.
The taut and easy wit she had to master
The brilliant talking fellow is gone. The trees
Are suddenly tall.

The lady is alone with all her flowers.
(What was it that the grass refused to hide ?)
His talk had charmed away the waiting hours,
And served to indulge her in a little pride
—But was that all ?

The lady feels the curl and lash of cold
Imprison her in an attitude of shame.
She knows already how it will be told,
Regrets not asking for the fellow's name,
And sees night fall.

LOVE DIES AS A TREE GROWS

What is it that begins, or ends, in this room at midnight ?

A tree grows in the dark. So we easily say : but which of us can conceive of the terrors and thrustings that ever-nocturnal growing and stirring to grow involve ? Who has heard the scream of the tortured roots ? Or felt himself drenched and drowning in the torrent of the sap ?

The wind brings us no answers.

Who has heard love dying in the dark ?

It dies with the same soundless scream as the tree utters in its growing.

We are all deaf to that scream.

The night passes ; and reluctant eyes see on waking that the tree is the same as on the day before, and the love is unaltered.

But, despite the sensual evidence, the gree has grown, as the love has died—only a little, but the growth and the death are both there, though we have not heard the scream of their process.

What is it that is beginning, or ending, in this midnight ?

The wind brings no answer, for the answer is already known.

Love dies as a tree grows : in the dark, softly, and with a terrible scream.

TRIBUTE

Strange things have happened in her ambient,
For signs been taken and misunderstood
By men in natural bewilderment,
Unused to such disturbing, timid
Of her contradictory demands.

This was inevitable. In what other way
Could she, the needed and divine,
Achieve her necessary and impossible ends ?

COMPLAINT

Why does the trouble of your sleep
Stir such reluctant ghosts
Whose ineffective pasts
You do not even pretend to weep ?

And why, so late, do you call
To join that company
Of scaresleep imagery
The ghost of one you did not love at all ?

A YOUNG MAN REPROVES HIS ELDERS

Bald witnesses observant of my plight
May make bland comment as they shake their heads,
Or tell me that I'll learn another use for beds
When you no longer can invade my night
Nor I keep up love-tussling till the light.

These, as they shift upon their stringy thighs,
Can cough whatever wisdom they may please
Or mutter covetous prayers upon thin knees
That I may find conviction in their lies—
You controvert their meagre proof love dies.

So I am chosen by and choose this love,
Committed to its struggle and delight.
Bald witnesses, who lie awake at night,
Neither your aching joints nor theories prove
That you yourselves were never thus in love.

IT IS NOT FEAR

It is not fear but knowing what to fear
Frightens you most, whatever you believe.
I ought to know : I bought the knowledge dear.

You will find out, this or some other year,
In saying this I don't mean to deceive :
It is not fear but knowing what to fear.

And when my meaning's made completely clear,
You will of course have further cause to grieve.
I ought to know : I bought the knowledge dear.

And then you shall regret the shrug and sneer
With which you take this warning I must give :
It is not fear but knowing what to fear.

I give the warning now because you're near
And I must try to tell you how to live—
I ought to know : I bought the knowledge dear.

And even though you still refuse to hear
The warning or claim your right to disbelieve :
It is not fear but knowing what to fear.
I ought to know : I bought the knowledge dear.

OLD MAN'S SONG

Children do not read the clock
Or stare in mirrors at their fate
Or care that dictionaries lack
The words to make their loving right
Said the old man as he took off his clothes

Children do not need to think
Precisely on original sin
Nor have they urges to get drunk
Or from this foul world to be gone
Said the old man as he took off his clothes

The child is father to the man
And if that man grow old enough
He may discover once again
The childish meaning of I love
Said the old man as he took off his clothes

And cease to read the brutal clock
Or stare in mirrors at his fate
And find what dictionaries lack
The words to make his loving right
Said the old man as he took off his clothes

LOVE'S TAUTOLOGY

All statements that I make may be defined
In philosophic terms as meaningful,
Tautologous, or nonsense ; but I find
That, having got myself this bellyful
Of love (begging the question now what love may be),
All my statements easily reduce
To one, the random universe to unity ;
And instantly my philosophic wits deduce :

To say *I love you* is not indeed to be
In any new or desperate category :
I love you is the first, and last, tautology.

SAILOR

Easy now on a beach, he notes the sea
(An old bitch once, angry to bite and keep)
As over-emphatic in vulgarity ;
And turns upon his side prepared to sleep.

Remembered tides at once roar in his ears
And ride him down beneath his frightened eyes.
Scrabble and gasp among the plunging fears
Betray the nonchalance with which he lies.

Easy on whatever harmless shore
The green ghost will not lightly let him be.
His blood cannot forget the salty roar,
The suck and gobble of the feeding sea.

Saltsick, seadriven, he abdicates his right
To be at ease with his old enemy.
Witness the longdrawn watches of the night
He drowns again in a remembered sea.

REMEMBRANCE

The time I expect was summer
Said the old man trying to remember
But I have completely forgotten the weather.

Her wishes were no doubt auspicious
Said the old man remembering his wishes
But I have forgotten if I gratified her wishes.

I expect it was a very happy season
Said the old man remembering the sun
But I have forgotten the affair's conclusion.

A LESSON IN CRITICISM

The poem reminded this one of a moth
Beating its fated wings into the light ;
While that one thought the lines a pretty froth
On top of nothing half as solid as broth.
Poor teacher had to show neither was right.

Somewhere I expect the proper moral lies :
Either—do not expose your poems in school ;
Or—pick on teachers that are poem-wise ;
Or—think conflicting readings are a prize.
What hope from readers when the poet's a fool ?

INNOCENT SONG FOR TWO VOICES

SHE

Shafted body in the sun,
When your work or play is done,
What is left of you to me ?

HE

Graingold body in the sun,
When my work or play is done,
Something of myself I leave.

SHE

Shall I laugh or shall I grieve
When you've done what must be done
With my body in the sun ?

HE

Laughter and grief for you and me
And what we sunlocked two have done
Are gifts unto the child I leave.

BOTH

Then we both must laugh and grieve,
For this witness there shall be
To show the world what we have done,
The graingold and the shafted one,
Body on body in the sun.

A PROMISE TO MY OLD AGE

Strut, arrogant frame, your pride of bones
Over this green stage while the sun is shining.
When the sag comes and your now so limber lines
Begin to blur and creak, and the complaining
Breath annoys the air your movements cumber,
Then you shall with no regret remember
How you, lordly, strode earth once
Like any rightful owner, and were pleased
To see tall trees reflect your arrogance,
And knew that nothing young could be despised.

Old age, my fatal friend I do not know,
Remember, when some young itch interferes
With your anticipated peace, I pray
You freedom from these terrors and desires
Of disobedient flesh, and promise pride
Only in glories that have long been dead.
Whatever song or madness your last lust
May farrow, blame or thank or curse or praise
This earlier brash hero if you must.
Only remember here his promise lies.

A SONNET INSTEAD OF THEOLOGY

God, as we know him in a world of fact,
Said the philosopher, *writing down a sum,
Is defining limit of his continuum.

This does not mean that God is mere abstract ;
But, if God should irrupt into a state,
Then chaos would begin.

                    (*The Christian cried* :
"*But I have seen my God, and know He died*
For me." And the devout Muslim : "*It is fate.*"
The atheist stoutly said : "*God does not exist.*")

While I, John Thomas on any faithful line,
Aware of many meanings I have missed,
Am obstinately uneager to resign
My right of disagreement or my hope
Even in hoping there may be no hope.

But know one thing : that chaos is a fact :
Therefore presume God guilty of one act.

*Cf. C. S. Pierce.

THE TIME OF LOVE

The time, the time, the time of love
   Says the clock in the bed,
Is told by the creaking of your knees
   And the drumming in your head.

The time of love you springily felt
   Was a time not told by clocks ;
And you did not hear in the welcoming bed
   The drummer who knocks and knocks,

The drummer who tells you the time of love,
   And measures it in your bed,
And announces its end with creaking knees
   And a knocking in your head,

By a clock that doesn't need face or hands
   To measure your despair
That the time, the time, the time of love
   Has vanished in the air,

The empty air, the air you hate,
   The air around your head,
The air that gives its resonance to
   The clock that shares your bed,
The air that feeds and echoes
   The drummer in your head.

THE CHILD AT NIGHT

Locked in the green house of the dark,
Where flowers pulse about him as they grow,
He rides the fearful engines of his wishes
Into the distance and delay of morning.

Astride his terrors he must keep delicate stance,
Or fall into the soft devouring mouths
Of night, the tiger with a thousand heads
Whom promises placate and dreams sometimes.

Better are lucky words which make night's fur
Lie down as when you stroke a cat.
But it is hard to hear words properly
And say them out again to listening dark
When ears are full of flowers roaring
And the prowl of night and the thunder of his wishes.

If he can only cry just loud enough,
The house of dark will crack and morning come.

THE LADY AND THE FIR-TREE
(*To Mairit*)

The storm without, the storm within,
To my true love how shall I win ?
Sang the fair lady.

O ride the storm, ride the storm
Until your true love keep you warm,
Answered the fir-tree.

The wind is high, the sea is high.
How shall my true love hear me cry ?
Asked the fair lady.

O raise your voice, raise your voice
Until your true love shall rejoice,
Answered the fir-tree.

My love is dead, my true love dead,
And his death upon my head,
Mourned the fair lady.

O no, my love, my lady, no,
True love and death you now shall know,
Sang the dark fir-tree.

POETIC RETROSPECT

I tried to keep the summer in my head,
   Words, wishes, double weather,
But when I looked in the hiding-place
My heart had drowned that summer away
And nothing remained but the echoing bone
   And a cold wind blowing.

I tried to put the summer in a poem,
   Words, wishes, double weather,
But when I looked at the empty paper
My heart had wept that season away
And nothing remained but the echoing pen
   In a cold wind blowing.

The summer will not stay in mind or poem,
   Words, wishes, double weather,
And what I seek in the hidden places
Drowned in the charity of my heart
And nothing remains but bits of paper
   In a cold wind blowing.

THE RING OF LANGUAGE
(*for Hildie*)

What we are aware of are concepts and representations. It is a world into which the speechless animals have no entry, but from which we humans, no doubt, have no exit.—W.J. Entwhistle, *Aspects of Language*.

And out of the ground the LORD God formed every beast of the field, and every fowl of the air; and brought them unto Adam to see what he would call them: and whatsoever Adam called every living creature, that was the name thereof.

And Adam gave names to all cattle, and to the fowl of the air, and to every beast of the field; but for Adam there was not found an help meet for him.—*Genesis*.

> That morning Adam named the animals
> And for the first time knew he was alone.
>
> Fur, fin, and feather, tusk, and hoof
> Paraded there for Adam as he stood
> Alone among them with his gift and glory.
>
> Each, as it stamped its pattern on the sunlight,
> Looked at Adam and received its name,
> And moving on left Adam all alone
> To wait for the next one to be named.
>
> And when the morning ceremony was done,
> Adam looked round and saw himself alone.
>
> A ring of animals made round him a horizon,
> But he was lonely in the middle of their names.
> Adam had named the animals and now
> The names themselves made Adam's loneliness.

The friendly animals were all outside
The ring of language where he stood alone.
They could not come within his ring of speech,
And he could not get out and go to them.
Their names themselves made Adam's loneliness.

Adam had named the animals and knew
His gift was also his despair for ever.
Adam and all the animals he'd named
Must live for ever separate and alone.

Adam had named the animals—Adam alone.

THE MONSTER

When the sea-monster came to visit us,
Grey harbour-filling bulk with hungry head,
Although our shuddering hundreds ran to stare
In terror on his glaucous length, or pray
Where the sea boiled around him to the shore,
We were not properly prepared for such
An advent : no virgins could be found
Of the right age to satisfy the beast.

Although enthusiastic citizens
Threw fat babies, doddering grandparents,
Nubile non-virgins into the broth of sea
Around him, the monster snorted once
To show his great displeasure, and withdrew
The enormous serpentinings of his body
Over the horizon, leaving the town to mourn
Its inability to make a sacrifice,
And wonder what it is we want of monsters.

GRANDPARENTS
(*for Knut Johansen*)

This is a house inhabited by the young
Whose laughter gives the air a sprightliness
That charms our many guests ; we are famous
For our hospitality ; the house is full,
So people say, of love, of graciousness,
Sweetness and light, the classic recipe
For all we understand that's not barbarian.

Few people ever see our grandparents :
Grandfather sitting with his lidded eyes,
A trail of spittle down his fallen chin,
His fly undone, a squat, strong-smelling man ;
Or grandmother shut up in the attic room
Screaming soundlessly at spiders
What she remembers of life's plague and damage.

Both are dead, of course ; but all the same
We keep the old man tied firmly down,
And grandma's attic room is always locked
In case he should destroy us or she warn.

FAILURE OF NARCISSUS

Ah, it was cold that water and a cheat.

After the first blue shock
It seemed that he was going down a street
Of water that would end in sand or rock
But not in any dream or any love.
He would have tried retreat
Into the air's familiarity above
But he could see no grace in such defeat.

And so he sank.
              His staring eyes
Mirrored the element and his surprise
That even water could not make him wise.

A WOMAN WHO LOVED TO LOOK ON RUNNING WATER
(*for Elizabeth*)

A woman who loved to look on running water
Tawny in sunlight or mottled by the moon—
It could not be we should forget her soon
Or confuse her with somebody else's sister or daughter.

I see her stand upon a bridge in starlight
And dream herself into the river's flow
Until it seemed the water ceased to go
And she was rippling with that dream's delight.

O woman who loved to look on water moving,
O dreamer on bridges and on the banks of streams,
If I can keep you for ever in my dreams,
I shall know much of water and more of loving.

NOT LACK OF CHILDREN ONLY

Not lack of children only
  Tethered these two apart
Where neither heard the knocking
  Of the other's heart.

A keener lack compelled them
  Not to cut the rope
They tautly stretched between them
  Without love, without hope.

Not lack of children only—
  What could not be denied
To these two lonely lovers
  Was the unsatisfied

Longing to be neither
  Together nor apart,
Not to hear the knocking
  Of either heart.

THREE SONGS OF A MAD PRINCE

I

I sent a letter to my love,
  Sent it late and early,
A letter to my love who lives
  In a distant country.

It was a letter written out
  In the heart's despairing,
Asking her who could not read
  Why love was disappearing.

I sent a letter to my love,
  But did not wait an answer.
In the middle of the night
  I dreamed of love and danger.

My letter came back from my love,
  Came back late and early,
Burning over mackerel fields
  And over seas of barley.

And my love who could not write
  Told to me who could not read
A story older than our love
  In a single word.

Now I swim in mackerel fields
  Or lie in seas of barley,
Writing a letter to my love,
  A letter late and early.

I post it to that distant country
    Where her single word
Murdered all the witness air
    And epitaphed my heart.

Letter, letter that I write,
    Burning to my love,
Tell her if she learns to read
    I'll rise out of my grave

And come to her in mackerel fields
    Over the seas of barley
To witness in the living air
    My love was late and early.

II

I saw my blood run down the stairs
    Like a river, all night.
My love danced on the landing
    In a red light.

I woke in the blue morning
    And saw the bloodless day
Wrap my love in a white sheet
    And carry her away.

My love was dancing in the air
    Gaily, gaily.
Look, she said, my steps are light,
    My heart is free.

But I stood on the landing
  In the red light,
And gave my bloodstained fingers
  A message to write :

O the blood, the blood is a river
  That runs away.
And love is a dance, a dance
  By night, by day.

The river of blood that ran from me
  Runs as I write.
But though you dance in the bloodless day,
  You shall not dance at night.

For I shall lie on the landing
  In the river of my blood,
And should you come to dance there,
  Drown you in that red flood.

Your delicate bones will make me pens.
  And on your skin I'll write
The song of the bloody river
  That runs all night.

I'll tie up the song with a loveknot
  Of your drowned and bloody hair.
I'll burn the song, my darling,
  In the red air.

III

I walked abroad in my kingdom
  With my lost daughter
To show her her heritage,
  Bright lands, blue water—
Lie down, lie down in peace, poor prince's daughter.

I said, This land is ours,
Tall trees, green grass, flowers,
Fat valleys, burly mountains,
Great rivers, cool fountains.
This as you understand
Is a rich, heroic land.
Our fathers here did deeds
Famous across far seas.
Here is all man needs
To feed him or to please.
Lie down, lie down in peace, poor prince's daughter.

As we walked boldly there
Jays mocked in my face,
Bats sneered at my hair,
Worms returned my stare.
Greasy rats in the grass
Slithered like snakes.
The fields were fenced about
With scrawny stakes
And sagging wires where hung
Bones that had once been birds,

Foxtails, staghorns.
An idiot's fumbling words
Lolled from his tongue
Where children dined on acorns.
Some wry and stunted trees
Scrawled gestures on the sky.

Weeds tangled our knees
Where springs were foul or dry.
We saw an old horse dying
In a dirty place ;
A ravaged salmon lying
In the cold water.
We heard the wounded crying
Of deer in the mouldy wood.
Carrion birds were flying
Where the tall nettles stood.
Lie down, lie down in peace, poor prince's daughter.

My daughter said to me,
Father, in your kingdom
I would not be a princess
Nor a woodcutter's daughter.
Father, in your kingdom
Of bright lands, blue water,
There is blight and sadness,
No heritage for me.
Father, let me wander
Across the beckoning sea
To find another kingdom
And a prince who loves me.
Lie down, lie down in peace, poor prince's daughter.

I walk abroad in my kingdom
    Without my daughter,
And look at her heritage,
    Grey lands, cold water,
And all that's left to say
    To comfort my daughter
Who has left and gone far away
    Over the water
Is, *Lie down, lie down in peace, poor prince's daughter.*

THE BEAST AT THE DOOR

1963

LUCKY JONAH
(*for Ted*)

IN MEMORIAM—FRIENDS KILLED ON ACTIVE SERVICE

"A MAN BORN TO BE HANGED CANNOT BE DROWNED."—*Old saying*

Cold comfort when the blue yawn of the sea
Crimped men for the voyage even Admiralty charts
Have not yet marked.
                    I saw a ship go down,
Quietly in the middle of the afternoon,
And thought, "That's one man will never play cards again
With confident fingers and goalscoring eye.
He loved football and cards and girls—but had to die."

And then to hear my name in a brazen bar
In Alexandria
                   (sailors in white duck escaping
From the copper sun and memories)
My name spoken by a schoolfellow
Who had come so far and—"Yes, sunk twice"—
And so was going home. And twelve months later
Killed by a motorcar in Newfoundland.
O ships we dreamed of when we both were boys,
And saw the sea once annually when the Sunday School
Charabanced us chorally to the gold coast
Of Wales and all our longings.
                  You indeed went down
To the great waters—and came back again,

Not once, but twice, and so one would have thought
Had earned the right to go back home and garden,
And grow garrulous with memories over beer,
But the car got you, certain as a shark.

O ships, o seamen,—convoys, brawls, and rum,
And offered sisters—"Nice girl, very clean"—
The mad, forgiven captains—"Clear Lower Deck.
I have to tell you that we probably sha'n't
Set foot on land again. Men, I rely on you."
The scalded stokers and the sick, singed smell.
Torpedoes—and the quick way down to hell.

Captain's Requestmen and Defaulters : "*Hang that man
Like Billy Budd. He sees a submarine
In the undershadow of every blasted wave.
Permission to grow ? Granted. We'll all
Wear beards in hell. Compassionate leave ?
Not granted. Let the woman have her fun.*"
Who hit the bo's'n in the pirate town ?
In the nostalgia of our rum we drown.

Drown—"*Is it better in the warm and classic blue
Than in the cold waste north where even the strongest
Cannot survive three minutes ? Anyway, thank God
We're not poor bloody pongos in the sand.
At least we've water, rum, and cigarettes,
Almost enough to eat, and—Battle Stations* !
Here the bastards come again."
The bombs drop like a mockery of rain.

113

I have seen the proud ships sail—and, broken-backed,
Or gaping bows, or holes torn in the side,
Crawl back to harbour or go down, go down
To Davy Jones's Locker like broken toys.
One day we caught a submarine, trapped like a fish
In the relentless circle of sixteen ships.
She ran the white flag up, and still our gunners
Pressed their automatic fingers
To make her run with blood. Later, we laid
The wounded on our upper deck—one was dying—
"Like a butchered sheep," I thought,
And though I tried for it, I had no pity.

Voices : *"Remember me, mate ? Had a run ashore
With you in Alex. once. We found a girl
And christened her the Nut-Brown Maid."*
*"Remember me ? I hit a gharri-driver once
Because he wouldn't let me have his whip."*
"Remember me ? I fell out of the motor-boat."
"Remember—" all the frantic runs ashore
With Jacks who are not jolly any more.
Alex., Benghazi, Tripoli, Algiers,
Beirut, Valetta, Famagusta.—
O ports and harbours of my sunken years.

And all of life a long survivor's leave
For lucky Jonah, spewed up from the maw
To wait and wait and wait for death.
The sea's a populous city—half my world
Is walking there, up home with mermaids,
Cold, picked clean to the white bones,
And braggarting to fish, "The Navy's here."

A small boy in a small Welsh school
Dreamed over books that he would go to sea,
Knew schooners, barques, and brigantines,
The names of sails and rigging,
Dreamed of being a captain, proud and almighty,
Pacing the quarterdeck, and taming
Weather and mutiny with eyes reflecting
Glitter of seas, the seas
Of all the world—he knew them all.
Dreams, dreams—and now these drowning memories,
Marine entanglements to dreams and five
Long years of waiting to be drowned.

"A man born to be hanged cannot be drowned."
Maybe. But I can hear ships' bells
Strike the melancholy sound
Of dead men's names, of sunk ships' names,
The lullaby and catalogue of the drowned.

RHIANNON

My daughter of the Mabinogion name
Tells me Ayer's Rock is ten times higher than
A house, and she, being seven today,
Would like to see it, especially
To ride there on a camel from Alice Springs.
She also says she wants to be a poet—
Would the vision of that monolith
Stay in her mind and dominate her dreams
As in my mind and dreams these thirty years
There stays the small hill, Allt-y-clych,
The hill of bells, bedraggled with wet fern
And stained with sheep, and holding like a threat
The wild religion and the ancient tongue,
All the defeated centuries of Wales ?

A RULE OF THREE SUM WRONG
(*for Ivor*)

". . . a rule of three sum *wrong*, thus : As the sweet smell to those
kind people so the Welsh landscape is NOT to the Welsh."
      G. M. Hopkins on "In the Valley of the Elwy".

No, the landscape never sweetened us,
Nor all our mouthings brought us nearer God.
But where those windy generations trod,
Archaic fathers nearly anonymous,
Their poor paths chapelled and precarious
Between defeat and dogma, their old God
Was waiting with his necessary rod
To show them heaven is high and dangerous.

What waits now in the historic rain
For those who've left the language and the land ?
Only the heart's willingness to understand
The centuries' inalienable refrain—
What God has spared you from his powerful hand
Is never yours to lose or find again.

THE WELSHMAN IN EXILE SPEAKS
(*for Brin*)

Being a boy from the hills, brought up
Believing that fornication is a sin,
Adultery abomination, what should I do
But fornicate until I'm caught, and then
Commit adultery in my dreams. *My* dreams
—You have to plough the furrows I have ploughed,
Or pick the stones off the bitter fields
Before they're fit for ploughing, all day, all day,
Or lift potatoes until your back is breaking,
And then go home to the grudged candlelight
And the green bacon—you want your childhood
Spent like that—and with the compensations :
An old man's voice like something out of Daniel
Making the Belshazzars of the tractors tremble,
Hills, like Mam's breasts, homely and tremendous,
Schooled wildness of sheepdogs, ponies stubborn
As myself, and each winter's killing snow.
And the capel, God in a little bwthin
Once whitewashed—but God in the voices
Of the mean, the crippled, the green bacon eaters,
The lead me beside still waters buggers, the wild boys,
The sin-eaters, and the godly daughters,
All of them suddenly in unison
In the ugliest building I have ever seen
—Pisgah I shall never see again—
All suddenly bursting—not bursting,
All suddenly startled into song, to praise
The god of fornication and the world we lived in.

Boyo, if you come from a country like that
You can talk to me of sin and related matters.

WALES—NEW SOUTH WALES. MAY 1961

Autumn was always cold, and so was spring,
In the country that I remember for ever
Despite this sun and despite whatever
Landfall luckily after my voyaging.
In that land it was always a hard faring
For men contracted to a brute endeavour
By their great taskmaster to what would never
Be more than a thin and bitter harvesting.

But here the sun is warm on belly and back
As I indulge in wine and memories
And hear above the long Pacific swell
Stern voices of my fathers saying I lack
Their faith, their courage, their black certainties,
And everything they knew of Heaven and Hell.

RUTH MYFANWY

Being the youngest of a poet's three daughters
You have this much luck, that you are nearly seven
Before your father turns his verses on you.
Will you, when you are seventeen, say, or twenty-seven,
Be resentful of your sisters who had more poems?
Will you say, "Thank God, he left me alone"?
Or, "Poor father, he really couldn't help it"?
Or even perhaps turn poet yourself,
And write impossible stuff like this
Called On being the daughter of a poet?
Or merely invert Ben Jonson's phrase
And boast, "I am my father's best poem"?

At least I wrote a poem when I named you
Ruth Myfanwy out of the Bible and Wales.

MR JONES AS THE TRANSPORTED POET
(*for Gwen*)

"And how do you react to exile?" Politely
They ask ; and remnants of my country courtesy
Make me answer politely, meaninglessly.

I say, "Of course, a poet is in exile
Anywhere, always." And that "of course" disarms,
Undoes them. They are politely satisfied
There was something they always knew about poets.

Or I say, putting on a bit more accent,
And of course prefacing what I have to say
With that disarming and dishonest "of course".
I say, "Of course, we Welshmen are exiles
Just as much in England as Australia."
And they nod understandingly and smile politely,
And think I didn't really understand the question.

How could I tell them, politely or impolitely,
That the only exile is from her bed,
From that visionary and impossible moment
When our customary involvement made
A sudden meaning we had not known before?

Exile, like love, is a word not to be lightly said.

LLANAFAN UNREVISITED

I took for emblem the upland moors and the rocky
Slopes above them, bitter parishes
Of the buzzard striking from lonely circles
And the ragged fox hunting the lean
Rabbits, and the starved preacher nourishing
A little heat from a hell that once had meaning.
I had thought to be a proud man and isolated,
Inviolate as my hills even in defeat,
Not easily marked even by the incessant
Savagery of weather, God, and my relations.
Small, maybe, but tough I thought and unendearing
As feg and able to endure weather
That smashes the great oaks and makes mud
Of the good meadows and destroys good men.

And now I live in the good meadows, and I have
No emblem except your body, and I am
Still a member of a narrow chapel, and a boy
From a hungry parish, a spoiled preacher,
Greedily taking the surplus of your sunshine,
And still afraid of hell because I've been there.

PORTRAIT GALLERY

See Davies, who hates his wife because
At least once a week she makes him forget
He is a deacon ; see Tomos
Who is married to the old language,
And resentful of everything English, especially
Money, which he needs ; see Isaac
Who seems to have an orgasm when he sings ;
John Pritchard, the blue-eyed, who looks
As if he takes every woman in the parish ;
Bill Beynon, with the accent dropping thick
From his lips as he denies that he is Welsh.

Turn to the women : see Mary Jane, tiny
And eighty, who's had ten children, and milked
The cows immediately before and after
Each birth ; see Sarah, who got lost once
On a mountain, and noted for her good works
Ever since ; and Megan, who has three children,
Two she thinks may be her husband's, little
Ifor she knows is not ; and Miriam,
Who has been going properly to chapel
For fifty years and never understood a word.

Look on this gallery, boy, and wonder
What these, your ancestors, would think of you.

LAND OF MY FATHERS

Some frosty farmers fathered me to fare
Where their dreams never led, the sunned and blue
Salt acres where Menelaus once made ado
Because Paris also though Helen was fair ;
And now this ancient sunburnt country where
Everything's impossibly bright and new
Except what happens between me and you
When I ransack your bright and ravished hair.

Always I feel the cold and cutting blast
Of winds that blow about my native hills,
And know that I can never be content
In this or any other continent
Until with my frosty fathers I am at last
Back in the old country that sings and kills.

MY GRANDMOTHER DIED IN THE
EARLY HOURS OF THE MORNING

It was cold in that room, after the cold hours
Of keeping company with the big, shrunk man
Who had been her husband, my father's father.
Her sallow face seemed peaceful as ever,
Her straggle of hair blanched into the pillow
—You would not have guessed at a body under the bedclothes.
Past tiredness, I was a boy, incurious.
A little woman was dead, a little old woman
Who had long confused me with her youngest son.
I did not even think, How small she looks.
And certainly had no thoughts for her life of labour,
Nor wondered how she who had always been old to me
Had once been whatever beauty the world has
To the old man I now led out of the room,
Out of the house, up the narrow road,
In the dawn he could not see for tears, taking
My hand in his as he'd done when I was small,
Both of us wordless against the dawn and death.

LATE SPRING IN WALES
(*for Pat*)

It was a cuckooed land going gravely
About green business, and the lambs unbound
From snow and terror bounced high and bravely
On the moving, holy, and always dying ground.

A wind blew, warm as loving, from the west
And the girls came out like berries. The old hedgerows
Were sprung and blossomed to life, and could not rest
Till the hawthorn was subdued by one torn rose.

It was a curt cuckooing and the wind
Soon turned and all the girls were gone,
But a good time in which we should have sinned
When the eloquent and searocked skeleton

Of Wales put on a sensual covering
Briefly to preach the dogma of late spring.

ANCESTOR, OLD LADY

You know that old and angry look of hers,
The one that disinherits you but compels
You to remember you must share her hells
As she shares with your unforgiven fathers.

Now at ninety, in her ignorance
Of any torments but the ones that burned
Her as she saw a true love torn and turned
To otherness, she lacks no assurance

That you, the small boy tautened at her knee,
Will too grow up to beast and learn to break
Whatever good thing you clumsily make or take ;
From you, too, takes refuge in her piety.

And you are wordless for her as you must be,
And know that even could you loose the words
That whirr and chatter in your mind like birds,
You would not. You regard her wordlessly.

Now, after her dead years, you are still not free
From her assumption and her angry look.
You can put down your fathers in a book,
But only stammer for her, unwillingly.

RELUCTANT

Yet heaven, since time began,
Loves a reluctant man.
VERNON WATKINS

I would make a sullen claim
To sit in those harsh pews,
Stretching the dry sinews
Of wit to learn a name
And slowly spell my shame.

Tardy indeed, and loth
To admit I could admire
Such a consuming fire
In which the one was both
Desired and desire.

Pulpit and pew forgot,
The only sermon heard
Mine upon the word
That is my own like snot
Or the sweetness of my turd :

I find in another land
Another poet say
The words I dare not pray :
God, take me by the hand,
And let me understand.

HEAD IN THE CLOUDS

Head in the clouds to you is a worn phrase
Weakly used to indicate disapproval
Of somebody else's ability to evade
Or ignore the day's burden and trial.

But to us who were born above Pencarreg
Head in the clouds is true, is simply true.
Nor all the brazen comfort of the sun
Can dissipate the clouds upon Penrhiw.

And if you say, as other friends have said,
That I walk always with my head in a cloud,
I am wilful enough to take you literally
And let your saying make me homesick and proud.

Homesick for clouded hills that never lose
The loom and shape they had when I,
My head in other clouds, trod their old paths
Too proud then to know that I too would die.

Proud now to know that when I have to die
My head has always been in clouds : first those
That still hang low over Pencarreg and Penrhiw,
And then the ones in which you shroud me close.

CWMCHWEFRI

I have been walking above Cwmchwefri
Where the hills slant sharply into rock
And nothing, not even a kite, hopes to live.

Up there, above even the last sheepdroppings
And bits of rabbitfur and peewit feathers,
I could see sickeningly below me
The sideland farms precariously
Clinging among the bracken to an old
And often defeated hope.
                                    You must believe
In some impossibly glorious promise
To mow meadows and milk cows in such
Unlikely places.
                            What will happen now
When they listen to the six o'clock news
Instead of bawling Alleluia
To their beautifully unjust God ?

STORMY NIGHT IN NEWCASTLE, N.S.W.

Rain thrashes the house, and I am back
Where such a ruffian night would lullaby
Me to a dreamless sleep. I lie
And listen to the wind's threat and crack,

And cry, I am not homesick, am not sick
For hills so sodden with such rain
And wind their absence is a pain,
A calm day makes us wish a storm come quick.

No, it is too easy to remember, now
When just a harmless lash of rain
Can keep me from my sleep, that then
I could have slept as sound as other men
Through better storms than this, nor wondered how
A sleeper in such storms would wake again.

OLD COMPULSIONS

Old compulsions, insistent as rain,
Distort our language so that we speak
In fashions manneredly askew, oblique
About the nurtured marrow of our pain,
Are scornful of the kingdoms we would gain,
Admit, mock-modestly, we have technique
But not there is a love for which we seek
On hills we mourn we shall not walk again.

The bittersweet of exile intoxicates
Us with a still more savage grief
Than when we abdicated from belief
And all the imperative ancestral hates.
And yet with bitter competence of tongue
We crow the hymns our fathers proudly sung.

IN MEMORIAM

". . . where you may see how God blessed husbandry in this land."
FRANCIS HIGGINSON, *New Englands Plantation, 162—.*

But not in mine. See Daniel wear the sky
Like a sodden overcoat, the earth weighing down
His feet, as he wrestles again with an old text
And wonders why his sheep are so obstinate about dying.
Sometimes, picking stones off an old, thin field,
Or riding, wet to the waist, through the bracken
In search of old, thin sheep scarce worth the saving,
His mind would be lifted from perverse sons and daughters,
His head kestrelled in space towards Allt-y-clych,
And he felt he could prophesy like Isaiah.
Or he would see somewhere towards Abergwesyn
The city that had no need of the sun, neither
Of the moon, to shine in it.
                    But always
He had to go back to the cramped house, to too many
Sons and daughters, unprofitable husbandry.
He would not have welcomed a more blessed land.
You can be terribly close to God in these places,
But what can he dream or prophesy in the jasper city ?

I do not hope that he would approve of these lines
Written in the new language, but I hope
That when I am an old man, as he when last
I saw him, I too can continue picking the hostile
Stones off my sour fields, and riding wet to the waist
Through the recurrent bracken, and still
Lift my head to sudden visions and prophesyings,
And thank God that he never blessed husbandry
In his own land—Daniel's and mine.

133

CWMCHWEFRI ROCKS
(for Madeleine)

In the cold splendour of that rocky place
I killed a rabbit with a stick, and stood,
Exultant, virile, dominant,
And ten years old. Next day I crept
To worship with a washed and Sunday face
The God who killed me like that rabbit. Sick
Now with longing, I wonder what I've kept
These thirty learning years, or understood
No rocky god can ever again supplant
The goddess who is nourished by my blood.

Apollo had never shown his face up there,
So far above the brown and troubled brook
Its fretting hardly broke the insidious mist
That was closer and colder to you than your bones,
And when you avoided her in masculine prayer
It was the buzzard Jahveh swooped and struck
So that your verse has murderous undertones
Like rocky faces where you dare not look
Now, for the bloody thorn with which he missed
Might mark you if you dared to read his book.

I killed a rabbit once, and once allowed
A proud demanding woman to ache and take
Me to her bed, and once I hope to write
On pages savage as Cwmchwefri's rocks,
A few lines triumphing and loud
That show that neither Jahveh nor Apollo
Are responsible for these intermittent shocks
That kill me over and over, and make me take
Her hand in my hand in the stormy night
—What the gods kill, my breasted goddess mocks.

Ceridwen, in your arms I can forget
Cwmchwefri rocks and the stern face of God
So that you come to me by night and night,
Blot out those images and those stricken cries,
And promise, promise that I may be yet
A poet worthy not to be refused
When you demand a proper sacrifice
Of running blood, of understanding blood.
Assure me Jahveh's nor Apollo's might
Assault your poet when for you he dies.

SWANSEA

Landor in Italy longed for an old bay
That even holidayers cannot spoil,
Smutch, litter, peekaboo it as they may,
Or violently rest there from their toil.

I would not walk now in that memoried town
In case I met the all too affable
Ghost of the wave's son, and with him drown
Happily saying life is terrible.

Drown in mixtures thinner than Mallarmé
Dreamed for Poe, but blacker in their way.
St. Helen's, Sketty, and Cwmdonkin Park—
O Iesu, what's there left for me to say?

Only that that old bay and that old park
Are there, as Dylan still is there for me.
No bloody air-raids ever rubbled away
The birdridden and sea-assaulted country

That belled our Dylan out over the bay.
Voice of the sea, and murmur of the land,
Bayvoice, seavoice, birdvoice, o silent voice,
Where you belong is all I understand.

PRAYER TO THE STEEP ATLANTICK STREAM
(*for the natives of Borth*)

Rhymes, ships, and winter—all a western sea
Howls that it holds them far, far away
While here the golden blackmail of the day
Holds me in winterless security.

How can I stop that shouting in my ears
Of the cold waves that batter on the rocks
Of Wales with the sound to which my own heart knocks
And all my fathers howling down the years ?

O ships, o winter, o remorseless rhymes,
Let me still howl against that western sea
The old cry of the defeated and the free
For all my fathers' eloquent times and crimes.

And, despite my surrender to the sun,
Despite my squandered lust, o western sea
Whose howl is in my head continually,
Permit me only do what they have done.

And so I may at last find a kind of peace,
And lie down with my fathers, safe from rhymes
And ships and winter and their storied times,
And even your knock and howl may still and cease.

III.   EROS

BEWILDERMENT

In a perhaps momentary confusion
I said I loved you ; but I did not know,
Flushed as I was then with the warm contagion
Of your flesh, how love could grow
To these proportions of bewilderment.

Now that the flesh grows cautious some old rage
Works yeastily within me. I had thought
It might be possible in middle age
To be less constantly distraught
Because of you into bewilderment.

That moment of my luck becomes too late
This time now when we might have been at peace
If either of us knew how to create
From our poor weathers of unease
Climates of unbewilderment.

NEVER AGAIN

Never again I said shall that invader
Come to incite the mutinous provinces
Of my blood : now I can look on women undisturbed.
Never I said, and stammered into silence,
For suddenly I saw your candid eyes.

NOT YOUNG ANY LONGER

The definition of being young
Is not believing in death as something
Personal : death happens to others.
The first whisper, warning, welcome, of age
Is when one says, I too will die.
One gets used to the idea.
                             Then suddenly
Your young breasts bring again
The illusion of immortality.

TO MICHELINE

It was that great man Thomas Jefferson
Who said that every travelled man
Asked in which country he would rather live
Would have two answers : my own, and France.

Somehow, as the years went by, I'd twisted
This into the equal truth that every
Civilized man is native to two countries :
His own, and France. It was my boast
Until I wondered if I still believed it.

Then I met you. And know for ever after
That, like the English queen upon whose heart
You'd find engraved the name of a French town,
My heart shall wear for ever now the Welsh
Red dragon tangled in France's lilies.

139

A QUEEN'S LOVER

Invested by you in that royal sleep
I woke to feel the old vexation
That even such love as we know cannot keep
The lineaments of love upon your face
When you go from me to another place.

But with such small things I must be content
After our royal hour of celebration :
What closed eyes, slightly parted lips, meant
In the uncertain morning's light and shade
To the naked victim of your accolade.

And how upon your body I have lain,
Upon your wild heart's perturbation,
Waking to know that I shall never again
Evoke from you that all too human cry
Or you from me that last triumphant sigh.

And when I go now in the common day,
Memory turning to imagination
Already as the passionate dark gives way
To dreaming light, my distant queen, you rise
To other lovers dawning in your eyes.

But this one gift you cannot take from me
As I cannot recover my oblation :
Whenever in the morning light I see
A woman's face beside me in the bed,
I shall remember you though you be dead.

SHE IS ASLEEP

Sleep recomposes
Your features so that one would not guess
Now in your nude defencelessness
The terror your waking face imposes
Upon your lover :

Terror that he might lose
Through lack of tenderness, through lack of tact,
Through some importunate act,
His dreamed-of, undesired power to choose
Between lover and lover.

SICK WITH REQUITED LOVE

Sick with requited love, your lover wonders
Whether upon his own dishevelled bed,
Waking to the sweat upon his pillow,
His flung arm encountering nobody there,
That loyal fever would have driven him then
To rise, take pen and paper, and write you
Better poems in that hour of longing
Than will ever be provoked by the piety
He feels for the satisfying nightmare
He shares with you now as he shares your bed.

TWO COFFEE CUPS

Two coffee cups as paradigm
Of two who would be one in bed—
We were oblivious of the time
And hardly conscious what we said.
The machine's contrapuntal hiss
Seethed in the cauldron of our kiss.

That kiss, that like the coffee cups
We could not take, but looked instead
With unintended downs and ups
Into our eyes which spelled out bed.
And felt the table melt away
Till there was nothing left to say.

Nothing to say, or do, about
Two coffee cups upon a table.
We paid our money and went out,
Willing and utterly unable
To reach love's right true end,
Scorning to call each other friend.

And now two coffee cups can seem
More than two cups, even more
Than what we hardly dared to dream
When we walked through the swinging door.
Coffee itself can symbolise
The desperate urgency of eyes.

Two cups, the same, and yet apart,
Together and terribly alone,
So obviously your heart, my heart,
Your flesh, my flesh, your bone, my bone.
Now I have nothing but this word
Which only you have overheard.

BETWEEN NIGHTMARE AND NIGHTMARE

Walking between nightmare and nightmare
I have grown accustomed to being tense
Against what unexpected violence
Love or not-love may demand I bear.
And though you make of me your nightly care,
Your arms around me as loving evidence
That such proximity is our best defence
Against the terrors of nightmare and nightmare,
My guilt is closer to me even than you.
Witness this startled hair, these shaking hands,
That when I am incautious and relax
In sleep, I am taken by treacherous bands
And in just flames am melted down like wax
—Between nightmare and nightmare I am tense with you.

A CONFUSION OF BRIGHT WOMEN

It was a confusion of bright women troubled
Me this morning between sleeping and waking,
The jargon of their names making a twittering
In my head and their too well remembered bodies
Making in mine the usual disturbance.

Olwen, and Blodwen, Mary, Jane, and Anne,
Megan and Deborah and Marguerite,
Came back like ghosts to stir my ghostly blood.
All honest housewives now, or maybe dead,
Though still for me causing this bright confusion.

And some indeed were daughters of the swan,
And others, though not beautiful, were merry girls.
Their hair of different colours, and their eyes.
Go from me now, trilling your tender names,
Forgotten girls I once was glad to know.

One had a mole like Imogen, and one
Was witty even in the morning, and one
Would sulk for hours, rejecting kisses.
How am I tangled still in those endearments
Murmured to your sweet and bygone names.

Comfort myself against this bright confusion
In this uncertain time between sleeping and waking.
If I should call you by some other name,
What matter so that I hold you rightly
And make this poem for you, only for you ?

ADAM'S SONG AFTER PARADISE
(*to A. D. Hope*)

And I remember how I named
The innocent beasts that came to me
And God said what I did was good
And for reward created thee
Torn from my side and fashioned fair
To be my hope and my despair.

How I have lapsed from innocence
Since first we lay and were as one
So that we now do furtively
The deed in open joy begun
And beg the favour of the night
To cover us from our delight.

And shall I blame thee ? Shall I blame
Seductiveness of hair and eyes
The promised welcome of your breasts
The long allurements of your thighs,
Say these are blazons of my shame
And know the heartbreak of your name ?

I take again your guilty hand
I look into your candid eyes
And am content that I have lost
That half-regretted Paradise
To win your human smiles and tears
To comfort my declining years.

A MIRROR OF HERSELF
(*for Jill*)

'*And Eve made air a mirror of herself*' WALLACE STEVENS

We are descended in more senses than one
From that bright mirror-making myth,
Comic inheritors of a tragic fault,
And the air is blue about us everywhere.
How fair she was whose daughters are so fair.

This you might think is the merest allegory
For some casual encounter of the flesh,
A sharpening of my wits on some bright bone
To disentangle images from hair
And praise her darkly whom I find most fair.

And yet—the blue mirror is a very fact,
And I am conscious of her dear descent
Reflected in my serio-comic eyes
As well as in the circumambient air
Informing us and her that she is fair.

And so give thanks for the original
Making the air a mirror of herself
And carelessly preparing our descent.
Praise be for fallen beauty everywhere,
Daughters and rivals of that original fair.

A BIRTHDAY POEM FOR MADELEINE

It was at first merely the inconvenience
—Children, we thought, would interrupt our love,
Our lovemaking, thwart our careers,
Interfere with plans for foreign travel,
Leave us less money for drink and cigarettes,
And generally be a bloody nuisance.

Then, almost without our noticing it,
There the three enchanters were, and we
Were more in love than ever, and we told
Childless friends to follow our example.

But now—three tall daughters growing taller
Every day—who am I to boast I bear
Such tall and triple responsibility ?
I should be frightened, I should run away
To sea, or to some childless woman's arms,
Or to writing poems in a lonely room.

Then I see your smile upon the pillow,
And, forgetting inconvenience, responsibility,
I answer as I can to your sweet asking,
And only hope these girls deserve their mother.

ON THE BANKS OF SOME RIVER OR OTHER

I heard the water talking like a woman.
It made me into a tall tree.
Go from me, from us, little fish and birds ;
Reach for your own sky, flow to your own sea.

Now that I am a tall tree above this water,
Gone the little fish and birds,
I would give anything if I could only
Understand her woman's words.

VETERAN

I

Young veteran, and still presumptuous,
Hoping still to win on the rough field
If not some silk or golden trophy to grace
My hard accustomed bed, at least
Some honourable scars—but routed
Even before the encounter—I would be ashamed
Were it not for the terrible kindness
Of your eyes as you forbade me even
To think of fighting, and sent me home
To sulk among the tents in glossy meadows
While the true champions killed each other
With fine disregard because of you.

II

Why do you summon me now the fight
Is over and all the champions dead ? Lady,
Was it for this you saved me ? Save your breath.
I am a soldier still, and I will take you
As a soldier, not a pavilioned skulker,
Take you as spoils, as plunder to be taken
And then thrown away. Despite your commands
I owe a loyalty to my dead comrades.

III

Ah lady, I am an old veteran now,
Without presumption, and need not be commanded
To stay thus, in this pavilion, with you, for ever.

NEVER

All night in the ready fields
   My love went running,
Looking for a likely man
   With all her cunning
To play catch her who can.

All night it was gay for her
   In the compliant grass.
Tall men tried helplessly
   To stop her pass
As she ran so ingeniously.

But in the cold morning
   As she tasted the dew
My love was caught for ever
   By you know who.
My one word now is never.

LOVE'S MYTHOLOGY

I have played so many rôles—swan, dolphin, lion—
In covering you, and still you can reduce
Me to this mere outraged despair
Simply at the thought of you lying naked there.

And this, no doubt, is love's mythology
And ours, but I did not want to turn
Your naked truth to words, not even mine,
Even though from myths poets cannot resign.

Turn for me then upon your naked bed
Warm shoulders waiting for me to declare
I am dolphin, swan, or lion, at command
Of your imperative caressing hand.

And thus we shall outdo mythology
By being nothing but our naked selves.
Think of me as lion or dolphin or as swan
So long as you are what I lie upon.

WITH THE SEA'S VOLUBILITY

Young man, lover, poet ; how easy to foretell
That for all of them the body will grow old.
Especially for the poet, conscious of other rôles
He must have played once, easy to imagine
He knows that he will savagely welcome the time
When in his old rage he will assault
The inevitable cliffs though helplessly.

But how hard to tell any of them, or yourself
In any of these rôles, that when you are middle-aged
You must storm helplessly against young beauty
With the sea's volubility but not its salt.

DARK RIVAL

Twin, dark rival, supplanter,
How I hate you in the morning mirror,
Punctual as midnight sweat,
All for the bright recurrence of her hair.

Though I can scrawl good verses yet,
You are as close to me as murder,
And I greet you every night in nightmare,
Every morning in the surly mirror,
Heedless so long as her bright hair falls.

It will fall so for my executioner,
My twin, my dark and doomed supplanter,
Companion of my sweat, face in my mirror,
Victim of her cool implacable eyes.

Midnight and morning I only prepare
In the intolerable shadow of her hair
Your usurpation and my sacrifice,
Of equal worth to her impartial eyes.

ONE MEMORY

The delicate and reluctant deer
Stepped and stopped a moment in our garden,
Nibbled at a frosthard cabbage, and then departed
With the same hungry dignity with which she came.

There were no hounds after her ; only winter,
Remorseless as God or parents ; and I was sick
For her boned beauty only for a little while,
And still do not dare to think of how she died.

But I know she died : the quick mouths of hounds
Would have been more merciful, some grace
Among that slaver and baying she could not find
In the slow sleep in the last drift she stumbled into.

And there, where houndtooth could not reach
Nor cabbagetop entice, there the bone of her beauty
Still whitens against the offwhite of bogcotton, as you
Still intrude with a bony gleam into my life.

IV. OWL AND ECHO

ON A PAINTING, 'SUNK LYONESSE', BY RAE RICHARDS

Perform is a word of which we forget the singular beauty. Its meaning is : to furnish forth, to complete, to finish, in a sense which is influenced by the ideas clustered in the word *form* ; so that *performance* is an enlightening name for one of our richest activities, rich with extra life. R. P. BLACKMUR

It was to make the words perform
I laboured, and it was to make the paint
Perform you toiled in sea-sunk Lyonesse.
And now we ride the ruffian storm
Of our distress, the world's distress,
By virtue of these words, this paint.

Recalcitrance of paint and words
Is now redeemed, and all the long
Submergence in the labouring seas.
Now we ride out the storm like birds
—Performance of consummate ease
At which we laboured hard and long !

Now we have made our work complete.
Now we have found the lovely form.
Under green arches once more drown
So that our labourings may meet
Where our two languages go down
To find and finish what we form.

THE SAME STORY
(*for Rupert Hart-Davis*)

Always, it seems, I wanted to tell, compulsive
As that ancient mariner, the same story,
Careless of my listener's response
Or consideration of my own shame or glory.

The same story : the one of which I had intimations
In childhood when a cousin told a lie
And I was beaten for it. Another version
Was war and watching my betters die.

And there were other versions too—that girl,
And perhaps those others, most certainly
The one I loved and most betrayed
By my failure to be anything but me.

But if you know better stories, or truer ones,
I might tell them as fairy-tales for my grandsons.

ON HAVING MY PORTRAIT PAINTED
(to Rae)

I

I sit, trying to look nonchalant,
As if I'm used to being a painter's model,
As if I'm paid or famous or beautiful,
And as I sit, while your small skilled hands
Make only a painting out of me, I am
Abashed, not only at my own inept
Pickers and stealers, but at my indolence,
So often satisfied only to think of poems.
> *In the mirror I see a face*
> *You have not seen in any place.*

II

Another sitting : and now it's you complain,
"Your eyes aren't right. There's something wrong
About your mouth."
     My eyes were never right
To see the colour and happiness of the world ;
My mouth was always twisted into wrongness.
Still your patient labouring hands transform
Them into something rich and strange.
But though I'd recognize it anywhere
> *In the mirror I see a face*
> *You have not seen in any place.*

III

Now I am hanging on the wall, the owl
Reminds me that our only wisdom
Is to know the labour and the love we put
Into our making. I have seen you work,
And now each day can see what you have made.
And this contents me. I do not need to ask
What does this portrait show of me to the world.
In the mirror I see a face
No one has seen in any place.

SEA-FAITHS

"Till all our sea-faiths die"
DYLAN THOMAS

In countries where no sea-faiths were
I would not wish to live,
Nor would I have my love
Walk in any but a spindrift air.

In countries where no rip of tides
Or battering of waves
Threatens, whatever moves
Moves behind dusty palisades

Where no sea-faiths exalt, exult
Mermaid and merryman
To salt devotion
In the waters' praise and lilt.

In countries where no sea-faiths were
My love would wither,
Death and the dust together
Take what came from glory and the water.

Let kiss be sacrifice and prayer
Now, that we never come
To any dusty doom
In countries where no sea-faiths are.

FALL OF AN EMPIRE

There were omens of course, but mostly unheeded,
And besides nearly always inscrutable
Even to those old mad mouthers who needed
Nothing to tell them that the implacable
Future is already here, was always here,
And that our only courage is our fear.

Now as we listen to the violent hooves
In the rain as intolerable as blood
Only the frailest certainty moves
Us to erect against that flood
A foolish doomed impossible barrier
That only serves to emphasize our fear.

Whatever it was that made us disregard
The omens or fail to read them properly,
The trampling hooves now bring us our reward.
In the smoky light of torches we can see
The axe and iron club swing nearer, near,
And our last comfort is articulate fear.

THE MOODS OF THE SEA

The moods of the sea I celebrate
Early, late, in all my sunken voices,
When the maw of the marrying wave rejoices,
Or when its treachery lies sedate,
All moods, all colours, blue, white, green, slate,
These are the matters of my celebration,
The moods and colours of all generation,
Fountain of birth and of man's glaucous fate.

Moods of the sea reveal our monstrous wish
To sleep forever to that lullaby
That rocks the whiteness of albatross and whale,
Desire fostered by the seabirds' cry
To admit that we are born of water and we fail
Until we die and worship with the fish.

MR POPE

Mr Pope, full of pain and fine feeling,
Walked down the ordered alleys of his verse,
In precise anguish as he went revealing
Writing and morals go from bad to worse.

He turned in a neat fury of indignation
His wit upon the dunces and their crimes,
Measuring the justice of his commination
In the balanced complexity of his rhymes.

How we could use now his pain and his perfection
When the stupid army's swollen even more,
And literacy has become a means of rejection
Of everything by which Mr Pope set store.

But Mr Pope today would be a personality,
And to the rigid harness of his pain,
Would have, for celebration of his mockery,
To add one monstrous insult, though in vain.

We should rejoice before the curtain falls
That once the ordered walks of Twickenham
Witnessed, despite the slobberings and catcalls
Of the mob, the meditations of this gentleman

Who knew about chaos in his little world,
And stoutly strove as he might against the powers
That have always darkness on darkness hurled
To obliterate Mr Pope's bright vision and ours.

OWL AND ECHO
"I am the owl and the echo"

DYLAN THOMAS

Night is transparent, and the mousing sounds
Blade its black meaning : undertake me now
You overpowers as these branches tent
Me where I hover wising for the strike.

Soundstruck, I leave the toppled branches,
Mousing down all the wordy heavens
To lap me at the bottom of my plummet
Beneath her naked and re-echoing stroke.

Listen : for in the branches I had wisdom,
And I am wise now only in my echo.

THE MINSTREL BOY

Out of invented countries, comic scenes,
Wearing a few real tatters of some antic
Dreams and passions, and a honed-down knife
Grandfather used for killing pigs or kings,
A pocketful of sermons, sixpennyworth
Of sins, the minstrel boy emerges into
The world, half-frightened, half-contemptuous,
And alone. Behind him lag his leman
And his faithful sluttish bitch, ready
To run or lie at his uncertain whistle,
To bark or sigh in speechless admiration
Of his unharped and incredible songs.

SIMPLY TO WRITE

To be magical, and yet direct.
To be sensuous as a girl's body, and pure.
To write, simply.

To use the one inevitable word.
To have a natural rhythm.
To write simply.

To pay homage, to exact
A proper modicum of praise
For writing, simply.

To not disgrace her, not
Offend one's fellow-sufferers,
But write simply.

If only in the blurred beginning
I had been warned how difficult
To write simply,

I would have gone on wilfully
For your sake trying
To write, simply.

Demand of me no more than that
For your sweet sake I learn
To write simply.

Reciprocal magic then, sensuous
And direct, shall teach us both
To love, simply.

LINES FOR A DOUBLE CHRISTENING
Miranda Tietze and Vanessa Stowell, 30 June, 1962

For nine moons cradled in grace,
You and you have assumed
Your bright and proper place
Among the doomed, undoomed
Crowd of humanity.
May we have charity
To pray for you and you, that so
Angels speak always for you as you grow.

LINES FOR THE DEATH OF AN ALCOHOLIC

No more stale rinsings of the sun
Shall cool and whet his pampered lust,
Nor the abasement of his tongue
Swell with accumulated dust.
A thirstier river drinks him now
Than all our licensings allow.

Morning shall not torment and parch
Him, fearful to sleep or wake,
Nor ambiguity of nerves betray
By wilful and beseeching shake
He burns with the consuming fire
That's fuel to its own desire.

Lapped now by deeper waves he lies,
An ague stilled, untwitching bones,
Taut tongue unswollen and relaxed,
And silent all hysteric moans.
Only the stink around his grave
Says, Here was one we could not save.

THE NIGHTMARE OF KING THESEUS

Blind days I ravelled unforgettable
Threads of unreason, stumbling down tunnels
Nearer and nearer to some urgent breath
Anticipatory of the moment when,
Dazed in the sudden light, I should stand helpless,
My dropped sword clanging on the stony floor,
Useless against pervading nothingness.

A MAN WITHOUT EYELIDS

A man without eyelids—I call him a man
Now, though then I called him a bloody Arab.
Nothing else has ever frightened me so.

One day in school, Mr—whom I worshipped—
Caught me opening my eyes in morning prayers.
(I know now why I wanted to know how the others looked.)

But Mr caught the enquiry of my eyes, and whipped me
Only with words—I could have borne the cane—
And he said how useless I was with my hands,

And therefore how much I relied on my eyes.
And now that I know my eyes see only one thing,
I am very frightened to remember, as I do,

That flagrant man in the sun without eyelids,
Not even begging, merely without eyelids.
Even in nightmares now I close my eyes.

TO MY MOTHER

A finch sang in the hazels
Thin above the thorn.
My scythe hissed drily
Through the headland corn
I mowed alone.

Seagulls made clamour
About my leaning plough
Bickering for worms
I turned up now and now
Ploughing alone.

A woman seemed a woman
In wood or meadow
In the hard young days
When with my shadow
I moved alone.

And God was a loud voice
More urgent than thorn
There in the stoned acres
Shouting to warn
Me, me alone.

No finch now, no hazel,
Only the thorn,
God's shout a whisper,
One woman alone
Cries I was born.

THE BEAST AT THE DOOR
(*to Brin*)

When the beast came to the door,
Amiably slavering, his paw
Uplifted as in salute,
I noted the burrs on his coat,
And the small thorns that clung
To the wilful clots of dung
He wore like medals, felt
The sweat reek from his pelt,
His friendly stinking breath,
My knees bent therewith ;
For all his looming size,
And his incongruous eyes
Small as a pig's, or mine,
I would have him as my own,
Blatantly in my house,
Bald-rumped, big-pilled, wise
To smell out my tricks
As he sniffed around for sex
Or murdered meat,
Mauled what he would not eat.
When the beast came to the door,
Ambiguous visitor,
Expected and casual,
Despite his grin and scowl
I was ready to welcome it
Until I knew those white
Fangs were for me, and shut
The door, too late, too late.

THE COLOUR OF COCKCROWING

1966

IMPROBABLE LAND

The lineaments of my improbable land
Show no contrition that an old excess
Is now economy when hate grows less
As conquering others still misunderstand
How we can, dangling, always from God's hand,
Sullenly careless whether he curse or bless,
Absorb from stone and rain the rage to express
What long ago from paradise we banned.

Far from that stone and rain, I try to say
How that incessant fall falls through my veins
And how my bones are hewn from that sad rock.
I give no keys to anybody to unlock
Mine or my land's heart. Some strains and stains
Are seen more plainly in this sunbright day.

'BUT IF IT BE A BOY YOU SHALL PUT HIM TO THE SEA'

—TRADITIONAL

The lecherous and griefless sea
Was always more beckoning than gardens
To a boy from bare, exciting mountains
Who would have been all green thumbs in gardens
And was so used to being bullied by mountains
He thought he did not fear the sea's oblivion.

The books did not tell me, nor your griefless flesh,
That oblivion can also be found in gardens,
Nor that my fear and clumsiness on mountains
Sought the sea's obvious oblivion
Because of some salt lecheries
Older than any mountains or gardens

I could know of, with only my green thumbs,
So clumsy in well-kept gardens and useless on mountains,
Itching for the griefless hills of the sea,
Glaucous and absolute mountains,
Only these fractures and twitchings to guide me
To oblivion, the last and salt oblivion.

ON RE-READING THE TWENTY THIRD PSALM

No uncompanionable divinity
Comforts me now beside these unstill waters,
Nor in this shadow do I want to shout green praises.
All the days of my life, goodness and mercy
Are what I believe of the parables and thunder,
But what I remember, under this rod, unprepared
At the table, what I remember, is a dead sheep
Stinking in what we called a meadow, a pastor
Gutsily taking more than a proper tithe,
And three crows, indolently flapping
Back to a rotten, thunder-riven oak
When I disturbed their happy rotten luncheon.

In barren or fallow moods, I am tempted to make
Poems out of such obvious materials : a god
Renounced, but not forgotten, maggotty sheep,
Dumb insolence of crows, a half-dead tree,
A family sprawling and bawling back
Through pub and capel for three centuries
And more, the family lie, the pastor's lie,
And all the lies that I have told myself.

But beside these unstill waters, as I walk
In the valley of the shadow and am not comforted,
I ask, What have maggotty sheep and pastors
To do with my daughters, who never knew my God ?

WELSH PASTORAL ELEGY

You could, I suppose, make some parable
About Dai, stone and story him in a way,
What the Lord giveth, and so on, but I
Don't believe in these sermons which I love.

The trouble is, I worked with Dai, year
After year : milk bottles round the town,
Torn timber lugged down cold and bleeding hillsides,
Wet, ravaged barley ripping the skin beneath the skin,
Kale and turnips cold gifts for fingers
Without feeling, cold and mudded rods of potatoes,
Maggoty sheep in August which you had to dress
Smartly in as long as you could hold your breath.

And Dai and me, through all the calendar,
Through all the bloody and the bloodless months,
Wordless antagonists, sweating against each other,
And still surprised we have never been charged
With that murder, when we quietly killed each other,
Slicing the tops off swedes with frozen fingers.

ADRIFT

Over there there are timid coasts
And the tamed land behind.
I walk the sea with ghosts.

Even the sun is brave
Over the tumble and haste
Of my populous grave.

I shun the foreign land,
Content to share the waves
With the ghosts I understand.

Companioned so by ghosts
I ride this burial sea
Away from the living coasts.

And so remain dumbfound
With the sound of the sea, and the sea
Of the sound I sound.

SPOILED PREACHER
(*to many contemporaries, and some in especial*)

Sometimes in the sweaty and stained night
The thought comes to you, thick in your mother's
Flannel nightgown and the drunken sweat
Of your father's dirthard shirt : Suppose,
You think, you had gone through with it,
Suppose a war hadn't come conveniently,
Suppose—this is the moment when your scream
Awakes you to your own sweat and dirt—suppose
You had let yourself be dipped in the Chwefru
(Below where the trout were, and where they washed the sheep),
Suppose you had learned from the ghosts of Christmas Evans
And Evan Jones "the man from Eglwyswrw".
And you lived now in a meagre manse—
How beautifully you would have been able to thunder
Against sin (meaning only one thing, that thing)
To your thin and sinning congregation.

Pastor you would have been, as stained with sheep
As your grandfather—but without his little book
Of identifying notches, or the means to make them—
Or your uncle (McTurk's man)—he had thousands—
Or your cousin who was properly called Cutter.

Pastor you would have been—and what a hypocrite
You would have been in the glory of the pulpit—
Hair flowing all over the place, and hellfire texts
All endlessly against fornication
To a few thin and avaricious buggers
Of both sexes heedfully laying up their treasure
In the bank and whatever they thought was heaven.

But now you are emancipated—suppose
Any of them should look upon you now—
You could stand their contempt for your Sunday drinking,
And your tenderness for girl students and secretaries—
They took Sunday School in their time, and for their reasons.

But suppose, suppose,
You had to preach a sermon on a thin belly,
Hoping the big farmer would spare you an egg or two.

I suppose
I would have been a pretty good preacher,
Getting properly hot against fornication,
And getting my eggs.

WELSH CHILDHOOD

Eating the bread of the world
In the thin rain of time
The child ignores the crow,
The stoat, and worm who know
What bread and child will come
To, crumble to at last.

In comfort on harsh rock
Or lacerated pine,
Never out of the wind
Or the thin nails of rain,
He thinks that wind the breath
Of the world he knows is truth.

A bible in his mind,
A pulpit for his mouth,
Should he seek further for
The absence of the wind
Or accommodating truth,
Life's wound without a scar ?

The crow, the stoat, the worm
Wait because they know
He will never be out of the wind,
As long as he has breath,
That breath is the truth
He crumbles to in the end.

WITH A DISTANT BOW TO MRS HEMANS
(*I. M. Tomos Jones Crogau*)

I've never cried
Because I had not bulk enough to fill the chair
Grandfather left me when he died.

Though all his care
Notched for keeping in the ledger of his mind
Leaves only bum's and elbows' greasemarks there

On his own chair
He left me when he died. And still I do not mind
That even then I never cried.

If he'd been unkind,
I could church out from this chair's emptiness
To show how much I do not mind,

Kick again those bars
Heels high off the floor, holding just legs together,
Or mark straight arms with famous scars,

Nicks of my name,
Old preachers, ungot girls, served cows, the always weather,
Or other testamented blame.

Grandfather, our predicament we share :
We have the nicked involvement of our name.
I try to fill your chair with all my shame.

TAFFY WAS TRANSPORTED

Over there, the hills of Sion
   Tempt with their peculiar light,
Eternal beacons to the pilgrim
   Stumbling in this southern night.

With his eyes on heavenly mansions,
   Treading where his fathers trod,
Knowing that he's even further
   From the comfort of his God.

But the pilgrim, stoutly faring,
   Keeps his eye upon the height.
He whom Jahveh once has blinded
   Never more shall lack for light.

And the way into Salvation
   Underneath the Southern Cross
Is no harder than the pathways
   Where his fathers found their loss.

Eyes uplifted unto Sion,
   Hands astray upon a fleece—
HE is surely a good shepherd
   Who will bring us to his peace,

And fold us in HIS glorious mansions,
   Safe from Satan, that old fox,
Singing, singing Hallelujah,
   Sweetly in HIS pious flocks.

See, from here the hills of Sion
   Shine more brightly from afar,
And the lost sheep find salvation
   Underneath a crooked star.

MY COUNTRY, MY GRIEF

Anguish is my country.
    I would not recognize
A land where only fair winds blow
    And the sun shines.

But the land where every wind
    Is the breath of guilt
Is home, and let the loud seas lash
    Wherever I have slept.

My paradise will be despair
    And the cold winds that blow
About the rocks, about your hair
    And the grief I know.

BACK ?
(*to R. S. Thomas*)

Back is the question
Carried to me on the curlew's wing,
And the strong sides of the salmon.

Should I go back then
To the narrow path, the sheep turds,
And the birded language ?

Back to an old, thin bitch
Fawning on my spit, writhing
Her lank belly with memories :

Back to the chapel, and a charade
Of the word of God made by a preacher
Without a tongue :

Back to the ingrowing quarrels,
The family where you have to remember
Who is not speaking to whom :

Back to the shamed memories of Glyn Dwr
And Saunders Lewis's aerodrome
And a match at Swansea ?

Of course I'd go back if somebody'd pay me
To live in my own country
Like a bloody Englishman.

But for now, lacking the money,
I must be content with the curlew's cry
And the salmon's taut belly

And the waves, of water and of fern
And words, that beat unendingly
On the rocks of my mind's country.

WELSH BASTARD
(*to David Jones*)

I was always defeated
My dad died at Camlann
And his dad at Catraeth

But I walked Sarn Elen
And helped to make Blodeuedd
And was Nest's lover

I was not absent from Glyn Dwr
Or the last Llewelyn
Or the bloody-minded Tudor

Look for me in the annals of defeat
Or now and again a bloody victory
Places like Agincourt

And always in the dark hall of Cynddylan
Where the eagle of Pengwern
Lifts his talon

And always before her bright face
Defeated, like my dads
Who died at Camlann and at Catraeth
For her bright sake.

ANOETH BID BEDD I ARTHUR

"A grave for March, a grave for Gwythur
A grave for Gwgawn Red-sword
A hidden thing is the grave of Arthur"
OLD WELSH, *The Stanzas of the Graves*

"*Anoeth* . . . refers to something difficult to acquire,
hidden, precious, a wonder."
DAVID JONES, *Epoch and Artist*

And my grave, when you make it,
Will be hidden too,
Because, although a common man,
I married a princess,
Precious, a wonder.

So I would have my tomb unknown
But, wherever it is,
Quondam and *Futurus*
Written on it
So I may hope when Arthur comes again
I may recover my lost princess.

THE HEDGESCHOOLMASTER

I walked with a bare mind
Between the rich hedgerows.
My urgent skin was prickled
By an insistent rose
While a rapid fieldmouse
Mocked my lack of a house.

Harboured in twigs a bird
Stirred up a song
My deaf ear almost heard
As I lurched along
Between the thick hedgerows
Intent on a rose.

A rose, a bird, a mouse :
The thin skin of my mind
Twitched in that hedgehouse
To know that I, though blind
And deaf and dumb and worse,
Could still know the curse :

To walk with a bare mind
Between a hedge and a hedge
And breathe like a mouse the wind
Of the bird's knowledge
That even the rose's song
Is not for long.

THE SOLITARY WANDERER

Walking alone with sentiment, his twisted stick,
He can knock bravely off this thistle's threat
Or sideswipe this frog for its reminding face,
And stride on, meditate, and not be sick,
Though all his history is with him yet.

He takes his ruminative path, stoutly armed.
The mountains are subdued beneath his boots,
And the lakes are open to his eye, and shimmer.
It is a landscape he has wholly charmed.
The earth he tramps on snarls with all its roots.

He will arrive at, and look on, tarn and tor,
And make appropriate remarks on rhymes,
Preening himself on his ability to scan,
Even spare a thought for the jostled corridor
Where the slipshod shuffle through their crimes,

The slum where mere people scrabble, scratch
At what they have of life ; he will stale and wait
More implacably than lakes or mountains
For what torn cloud of joy he can catch
As railways, people, intrude, intimidate

His stalwart hiking out against the thistle,
The evil eye of the toad, the thorns and burrs,
All those small and inappropriate
Enemies, owl's hoot, finches' whistle,
Or the drawn, hinged grinding of a gate

That warns him in the dialect of men
Stout sticks and boots tread, thrash, earth, air, in vain :
Thistles and toads dislike poetic men.

BUILTH WELLS

A picture of a town beside a river :
Schoolcaps, girls' knickers, French letters,
And French teachers, beside the sylvan Wye :
How beautifully my memories lie.

Builth, Buallt, spa of no renown,
But sprawled about the grassy Groe,
Along the brawling reaches of the Wye,
Where I'll go home to die :

Small town, home of a great footballer
And of a greater choir, O Builth.
Stay small beside my memoried Wye
Where all my poems lie.

THORN

The thorn is punished by the October wind
And by the wind of March,
Companion for a bitter mind
And the blood's dark.

The thorn through all its punishment
In March and in October
Would not have any wind relent,
No mercy ever.

This is the prayer of the bitter mind
In the bloody dark :
May I be relentless in the wind
As the thorn, as harsh

As the punished thorn,
The thrashed and lonely thorn.

MOUNTAIN DEATH

An old reticence of mountains
Stripped and maculate
Reassures late
More than gauzy fountains
That tinselly sung
To us when we were young.

It keeps in the wind residual
Faith that to be born
Is to wear a keen thorn
Without any renewal
Of bone or sinew
Until death is due.

Death is good on the taciturn
Mountain, in the wind
More close than a friend ;
Under a familiar thorn
Pay for your birth
On unrequiting earth.

WORD IS ALL

I slur through the dingle, cwm,
To home in the wind,
A bare pine twisted above
A stumbled wall.
A word is all.

I try a bare poem, old
Like pine against winds,
Poem like where the cwm ends
Out on the hill
And word is all.

Could I make that bare poem,
True as home,
I could sing through the cwm,
Not slur, not fall,
Word being all.

But : twisted, winded, slur
All words, stumble the cwm
Wordbeat to home,
Slur and fall
The word is all.

MY GRANDFATHER GOING BLIND

When the cataracts came down, he remembered
Verses, grew grumpier, but did not cry or break.
His bulk sagged, shrunk a little ; he would have liked
The comforting presence of Mari, even as she was
Those last years, tiny woman in a big chair,
Talking mostly to her small boy sons, though
Sometimes she came back to this world for a moment.
When the cataracts came down, he remembered.
Was sometimes peevish, liked to talk in Welsh,
Was for the most part content with his old dog,
Blind, deaf, rheumatic, and pretty daft,
His firm stick, strong pipe, his memories—and me :
His grandson who could not speak his language,
Lacked his mountain skills, but in whom
He had a thorny faith not to be beaten
Down by any wind or language.
When the cataracts came down, creeping
Curtains over his shepherd eyes,
He talked to me.
                    The old names still resound
For me of farms, men, ponies, dogs,
The old names that are all that I possess
Of my own language, proud then
And prouder now to call myself only
Young Crogau, old Crogau's grandson.

I remember when the cataracts came down.

FOR MY GRANDFATHER

Ballad the idiom of my ancestry,
The beginning men on the hills of speech,
Old pulpitwalkers, pathtakers in every
Wind that brought a weather from God,
And brought me out of Brecon to this talking.

Sermoned among their troubled consonants
On Allt-y-clych the dictionary of vowels
Is always open at Alpha and Omega,
The tongued wind turns the pages of a Bible
To mark my birthday in Llanafanfawr.

No fire spoke to me out of a thornbush,
No true Book preached or pleached me on the hills,
I went down to the sea, to the great waters,
Rhymed in the antipodes of language,
But talk with a shepherd in the winds about Cwmcrogau.

A STORM IN CHILDHOOD

We had taken the long way home, a mile
Or two further than any of us had to walk,
But it meant being together longer, and home later.

The storm broke on us—broke is a cliché,
But us isn't—that storm was loosed for us, on us.
My cousin Blodwen, oldest and wisest of us,
Said in a voice we'd never heard her use before :
"The lightning kills you when it strikes the trees."
If we were in anything besides a storm, it was trees.
On our left, the valley bottom was nothing but trees,
And on our right the trees went halfway up
The hill. We ran, between the trees and the trees,
Five children hand-in-hand, afraid of God,
Afraid of being among the lightning-fetching
Trees, soaked, soaked with rain, with sweat, with tears,
Frightened, if that's the adequate word, frightened
By the loud voice and the lambent threat,
Frightened certainly of whippings for being late,
Five children, ages six to eleven, stumbling
After a bit of running through trees from God.
Even my cousin who was eleven—I can't remember
If she was crying, too—I suppose I hope so.
But I do remember the younger ones when the stumbling
Got worse as the older terror of trees got worse
Adding their tears' irritation to the loud world of wet
And tall trees waiting to be struck by the flash, and us
With them—that running stumble, hand-in-hand—five
Children aware of our sins as we ran stumblingly :
Our sins which seemed such pointless things to talk
About to mild Miss Davies on the hard Sunday benches.

The lightning struck no trees, nor any of us.
I think we all got beaten ; some of us got colds.

It was the longest race I ever ran,
A race against God's voice sounding from the hills
And his blaze aimed at the trees and at us,
A race in the unfriendly rain, with only the other
Children, hand-in-hand, to comfort me to know
They too were frightened, all of us miserable sinners.

II.

COTTON MATHER REMEMBERS THE TRIAL
OF ELIZABETH HOW :
SALEM, MASSACHUSETTS, 30 JUNE 1692

*Mather's righteous indignation that such things could be was uncon-
sciously submerged in the thrill of having been present as spectator at
a collision between heaven and hell . . . So far as he was concerned,
the delirium might begin again with full force tomorrow.*
          —MARION L. STARKEY, *The Devil in Massachusetts*

I

My duty to set down, to propagate,
Assisted by its author, its holy author,
And by truth's conscience as the truth requires,
The wonders and the wonderful displays
His infinite power, wisdom, faithfulness,
And goodness hath irradiated this
Indian wilderness with, the wonders
Of Christ's religion fled old Europe's
Deprivations, to raise the New
Jerusalem on a barren strand,
And in the wilderness to reap choice grain.

So many memorable occurrences, so many
Amazing judgments and amazing mercies
Upon particular persons in New England,
My pen blazes its trail upon the paper,
A blinding witness of light towards Christ.

My bent's for praise—I hate those folio-writers,
Bigots for whom a contrary religion
Suffices to defame, condemn, pursue
With thousand calumnies—I hate with all
My heart such foul bias to obloquy.
And how commend what is commendable
Without commending ?
                         But I would be
Impartial too, accounting of events
With praise or blame according ; agreeing
With Tacitus despite Tertullian who called
Him the lyingest historian : the chief task
Of history is to record, as I have done,
Men's Christ-given virtues, and instil
The fear of sin and infamy, of evil
Words and deeds.
                         Even in the best of men,
Even in my friends, are many censurable
Things. I cannot forbear to censure,
Though I keep my censure sparing, more easy
Than my commendation. I have no wish
Vices and villainies to commemorate ;
So some unuseful things have properly
Left to oblivion, while I praise all good.

II

Back in the spring I preached a sermon
Upon Temptations. Summer was doleful :
My poor country wholly entered into
Temptations ; Heaven's dreadful judgment,
Here in Salem and in adjacent places,
Allowing the Devils bodily possession

Of many people, so that there seemed to be
An execrable witchcraft abroad,
And many were accused.
                    I can hear
The horrid cries from houses of poor people.

For my own part, I always was afraid
Of condemnation on feeble evidence
Of spectral representings, and testified so
In public and in private, and urged the Judges,
And wrote the Ministers' Advice, that they
Should by no means admit such evidence.
But I also knew the Judges, most of them,
Admired their patience, prudence, piety,
And saw the agony of soul with which they sought
Heaven's direction ; compared them with
Those others whom the increase of distress
Enchanted to rail and rage, to a scandalous,
Unreasonable disposition.
Though I could not allow some principles
Some of the Judges had espoused, their persons
I could only honour, and said so ;
Could only compassionate their difficulties,
And said so, here in Salem, the chief seat
Of these vexations from the Devil ; wherefore
The mad people through the country
Reviled me as a doer of hard things,
A prosecutor in the time of witchcraft,
Though in the beginning of the Evil-Time
I had offered (none of my revilers
So courageous or so charitable),
To try without more bitter methods prayer
And fasting to end these heavy trials
Of these possessed people, scattered from each other.

III

That June day in the court at Salem I saw
The conflict and collision of Heaven and Hell,
The Indictment of Witchcraft against Goody How.

The depositions first of those afflicted
By sensible and evident witchcrafts laid
To the prisoner's charge. Some were not able
To bear her looks, and in their greatest swoons
Could tell her touch from that of others. Some
Testified the shape of How gave trouble to them
Ten years before. Others were visited
By ghostly apparitions that pretended
They had been murdered by this witch, this How.

At Ipswich, upon suspicion of witchcraft,
She was denied admission to the Church,
And preternatural mischiefs followed.
There was Joseph Safford's wife. When How took her hand,
And talked of scandal and of evil report,
Even like one enchanted, immediately,
Unreasonably, and unpersuadably,
She took this woman's part, saying "Though men
Condemn you, before God you are justified".
Thinking that How was a precious saint of God,
Raved, raged, cried out, being taken frantic
In strange manner. But afterwards she fell
Into a trance, and coming to herself
Cried out she was mistaken, bewitched by How,
Afflicted by the shape of How, enduring
Many miseries from that, not to be well again
Till there was testimony for How to take her
Into the Church, sorry to see her husband at that meeting.

Others told of cattle bewitched ; of an ox
Choked with a turnip in his throat
At How's desire ; of cattle leaping three
Or four feet high in the air, turning about,
Squeaking, falling, dying, as How wished ;
A horse preternaturally abused ;
Of Goody Sherwin's difference with How,
Upon her deathbed charging How's hand in her death ;
And others told of unaccountable
Spoilings and spillings of their barrels of drink ;
Another of being taken with a very strange
Kind of a maze from eating of How's apples.
And Isaac Cummings, who had refused to lend
His mare to How, found the beast much abused,
Being bruised as from much running over rocks,
And marked as if she'd worn a red hot bridle ;
And when one went with a tobacco pipe
To cure her, a blue flame spread and burnt on her,
Flew upwards to the barn roof, and was like
To have had the barn on fire ; and the mare died.
Perley and his wife had differences with How :
Their cattle suffered ; their daughter was struck down
Whenever How was spoken of. She charged
How to the very death, and said she might
Afflict, torment her body, but could not hurt
Her soul ; the truth of all this matter
Would appear when she was dead and gone.
And penitent witches came to affirm that How
Was baptized with them by the Devil
At Newbery-Falls, having before been made
To kneel on the river's brink and worship him.

IV

These things in themselves were trivial, God knows,
But there being such a course of them,
The more they were considered. For the great
Part of the Summer, every week I spent
A day in fasting, alone with God. I cried
The Lord for preservation from the power
And malice of those bad angels, and the good
Issue of those calamities wherein
The miserable country was ensnared
With His permission by those evil angels.
I besought the Lord, I cried unto Him
To please to accept, direct, and prosper me
In publishing such proper Testimonies
As would be serviceable to His Interest.
I went unto the prison and preached therein
To those committed there upon suspicion,
Preached a sermon on a text from Acts,
Reasoning of righteousness and temperance
And coming judgment, helped by the Lord's Spirit.

That a right use be made of these stupendous,
These prodigious things, I have committed
Them to a book and published it, announcing
These wonders of the invisible world, and how
We fought the Devil here in Massachusetts.

V

The horns that sounded across Essex County
At midnight, the unaccountable mazes
In which men and women and beasts were wildered,
All the afflictions and torments, the agony
Of those who judged those who were only tried,
God's guidance for which I so strongly cried—
Were these things here in Salem ? Did help come ?
Is God's good wilderness now purified ?
Or must we fear and go in constant sorrow
That we are still afflicted, that tomorrow
May bring back to Salem that delirium ?

Note : I have taken some liberty with Mather's language (see
The Wonders of the Invisible World, 1693, and his *Diary*)
and have anachronistically used some phrases from the
Magnalia Christi Americana, 1702

EXCUSE
(*for Marlene*)

I blame it all on those headhurting books :
 The dreams and journeys,
Destructions, idylls, time's ambiguous mercies,
 And whatever looks
Like my revenge on what I found in books.

I blame it on the novels and the plays :
 Murders and marriages,
Visions and sermons, symbols, images,
 Those heady days
I ranted like the heroes of the plays.

I blame it on the poems above all :
 From that contagion
Comes the paradox of my condition :
 When I have blamed it all
On poems, it is the poems save me after all.

TO TED RICHARDS

Askew a bar, aslant
With your tall charm, you asked
"Don't you feel afraid
To see all your faults
Assault you in your children?"

Then, my one child only
Had temper. Now, I know
What you meant, and try
To keep quiet as they trample
Thoughtfully on my grave.

By God, we live, boy,
In some short memories,
Tall children, and some
Writings that are not
Better than they should be.

ON RE-READING OLD MYTHS

So you sit down, lean and slippered, expecting
A pleasant hour or two, more interesting
Because more reminiscent, than the latest fiction
Whether Who-done-it ? or I-won-the-war.
Certainly—you've dined today, and your mind
Is easily random, picking up pebbles here
And there on the edge of the great ocean—
Certainly you don't expect or want
A shock like that young Keats sustained from reading
Chapman's Homer, you have no desire at all
To feel like stout whoever it was
Silent upon a peak with wild surmise.
You only want this lapping silence (family asleep)
And these old stories to read instead of new ones.

Then how forgive her for this startled hair,
This sweat and shake, this more than hopeless
Recourse to the hidden bottle, this rabid
Ingurgitation of barbiturates ?

How can you forgive her that you cannot
Tell her what you cannot tell yourself ?
It was your grandam straddled in that wooden
And accommodating cow : it was your daughter
Languished naked on the water's brim
For the swan's glory : your mother
Who drove that man to tear his eyeballs out :
Your wife for whom they waged those bloody wars,
Uselessly on the windy plains, and burned the town.

So you sit down, forget psychology,
Reach for the bottle, take too many
Barbiturates, and sweat a few more hours,
Recusant, remembering favourite stories.

THE SECOND CRITICAL ENCOUNTER
(*to Marlene*)

You said, looking at some poems, ' These are good ',
And while I liked that, I discounted the friendly
Warmth of your voice—(' Bloody liar ', a voice says,
My voice,—' All right, boy, I see what you mean ',
I meanly reply in the same voice, almost.)
But you went on, ' Because here I do not see
The poet watching himself write a poem '.
And I realised that this is perhaps the thing
I've been trying to do these 'prentice decades,
To stop that, simply to write poems
That are good enough to be anonymous,
And failing always, because on the touchlines
There has been the too obvious figure
Of the boy who once wrote a beautiful poem
And has ever since watched himself do it again.

And though I've failed again in this effort,
And can see myself watching myself looking
—In optics there is no end to the series—I hope
You believe, as I do, I really mean
These mumbled thanks are for showing me the way,
Or at least for telling me there is a way.

SAWMILL INCIDENT
(*to Alan Mullard, Timberman*)

Look, I tell you he let that bloody saw
Take his finger off. I was there,
I witnessed it. Accident ? Keep that talk for the compo.
Boy, I saw him let that saw go
Just one burr—like that—and him there then
Holding up his hand, and the blood
Was everywhere. We all felt pretty sick,
Applying a tourniquet, ringing the ambulance,
Ringing his wife—I had to do that.
Fingers, of course, are often lost in sawmills.
I felt pretty sick about his, though.
Oh, he'd always been impetuous, but who'd have thought
He believed in sin enough to make the saw
Take away the finger that started the trouble ?
You don't believe me ? I had to tell his wife.
Pretty difficult to get that finger caught on a saw.
And the silly bugger's trouble still remains,
As all three of them know. Watch your hand there, boy,
These saws sometimes reach out and get you.
Don't you want any more fingers left than I've got ?

IN THE SHADOW OF YOUR HAIR

A stammering repetition of your name
Can jerk me out of any waking nightmare,
So that I can believe your eyes still shine the same
And your hair is unequivocally your hair.

Permit me stammer with my voice and hands
A little longer : homage, thanks, and prayer :
So that your listening body understands
This is my curse and cure and care
By lamplight and starlight and moonlight
It is your bright hair's shadow by which I write.

And, writing in the shadow of that hair,
I say old sayings over and over again
Without much reference to here or there
Or now and then, still less to loss or gain
—I only hope that you can read me right
When I remember that even your shadow is bright.

EYES, HAIR, SEA, FALL

Having in mind that ambuscade of hair,
I averted my eyes, but to a blank avail.
Spindrift of your approach assailed me there
To fall before I felt myself to fail.

Argosies I ransacked then, astride
The bright main of the fallen world, to seize
O buccaneering looks into your wide
And unforeboding eyes, salt promises

To deny sere leaves and all that fall
Into the deeper and the greener deeps
Where my fault could answer to your call
To sleep satisfied so where your fault sleeps.

Now I inherit my kingdom, the bonestrewn
Bottom of the sea my bones knew before
The green sounds out of which they were hewn
Or dreamed of lying safe on some dry shore.

Eyesockets bequeath this upturned stare
To the ambush of your hair, your drowning eyes.
O queen of darkness and the falling air
Look on your ambushed lover where he lies.

Not that you should know anything of despair
Or care he is so fallen from your eyes
But that the tides and ambush of your hair
Ripple in triumph over one who lies.

ON A DAUGHTER
(*for James Mc Auley*)

My father's scowl, grandfather's scowl,
Just as I have transmitted it,
On this face now
Evokes a likelier kind of grace
Than was to be expected from
Such a filial deviation.

Do lovelier lineaments disguise
In her the long-nursed guilt
The family scowl
Is signature of, the carried shame
We could not do without nor felt
At home if we were lacking it ?

What sort of hope I cannot help
Then makes me want to see that scowl
On the otherwise innocent
Face of a boy whose accusing eyes
Will call me grandfather and deviate
Perhaps into a path I left too late ?

A SMALL VISION OF HELL

Lipless, breastless, they importuned me with
Their tiny minds, huge hearts, tenderly
Telling me this was true love, I could forgive
The blind denial of their hairy parts.

Don Juan-like I stood as at command,
Slavered at navels, armpits, nipples,
Welcomed the cold rejection of a hand,
And sweated out my sentence.

                              Apples,
Red and gold, rottenly promised to fall.
The girls lisped sweetly this is true love we make.
The last thing I remember before waking,
I'd turned aside to eat the hairless snake.

RECRIMINATIONS OVER

Recriminations over, what's to do
Except what we have always done,
Tear at the unhurt flesh and leave
The mind, some minutes, alone
As will be, after all our thrash and grieve
The unrecriminating bone ?

A SAILOR WHO READS BOOKS
SENDS A CHRISTMAS CARD
TO HIS DEAD SWEETHEART
(*for Anna*)

Christmas again—shall I decline ?
(Do I decline ?) I do declare
Those voices in the springing air
Are always harder to define
When once again the shuddering whirl
Defies me to announce
Anything else that happened once.

O hang me on the Christmas tree
Anything's better than going to sea.

Once and once alone beneath
A still and perfect toy-hung tree
I was you and you were me
Until we died for lack of breath.
But now with any other girl
I keep on breathing to the end
And think about my sailor friend.

O hang me on the Christmas tree
Anything's better than going to sea.

Darling, in that private place,
Do you hang toys upon the trees
As you used to hang your breasts to please
My unaccommodating face
And what you only saw behind
My sea-washed and Platonic mind ?

O hang me on the Christmas tree
Anything's better than going to sea.

I take again my Christmas leave
—Of you, and Christ, and everything—
And all the bloody bones that sing
About me as I reel and heave
My guts up in the gutters of this town
Say, Sailor, go to sea and drown.

O hang me on the Christmas tree
Anything's better than going to sea.

PETRARCH DID NOT WRITE LIKE THIS

I stayed too late : my waiting was too slow.
You came, but could not wait my coming late,
And when I came could only bid me go.

I came too late : for you who could not wait
To tell me that sometimes I am too slow
To come to tell you that I cannot wait.

Now I am always waiting, waiting so
I may not be with you again too late
To come to you as only your hopes know.

Let me then, stay and wait too late, too late
To stop you coming to me in the way we know.
I stay for you, my dear, I stay and wait

For you to bid me to get up and go.
For you I come and make my coming slow.

ANOTHER LOVE

I straddled the world
And was not welcome.
I recoiled, curled up,
And was at home.
But who unleashed those singing stars
That bound me for my holy wars ?

I strutted up and down,
Nobody flaunter.
I played, I displayed,
I was a bold venture.
But who called off those startling hounds
That licked and lapped my singing wounds ?

I lay still as a mouse.
I breathed my own grave.
Not a woman nor seed could rouse
Me. I did not love.
What worm, what seed, what love was it that sang
To make these risen bones together clang ?

I died into another grave,
Another love.

'HERE IS THE PEACE OF THE FATHERS'

—HART CRANE

Drowned meadows, submarine
Shadows, lapsed bones in the swell,
Old talkers who now talk ghostlily well
Between one green and another green,
How my bones feel that your bones do well.

Peace, fathers, peace.
Talk, and may the peace where your bones dwell
Requite in all green undertows
The bitter overtones
Of my unpeaceful bones.

DISORDERLY SPRING

Disorderly spring once more
Beats its loud drum
And lewdly we have come
To the taut stretch of welcome
With our bloods' roar.

Borne on the genial tide
We abdicate our sense
Of pride and diffidence,
Roiled in the nonsense
Of the warm flood we ride.

The riot of this newcomer
Blurs and blots out all
Foreboding we shall fall
Soon to the beat and maul
The dry bruise of summer.

Disorderly days deny
And the unsleeping nights
Hysteria of delights,
Pleasure of gasps and bites,
Come to winter to die.

TOWARDS A HOMAGE TO
NORMAN TALBOT

A gentle man in a long wind
—Think of him as tall
To the accost of eyes,
Demure measure.
The fat wind wraps its rhymes about him.

He would go gravely.
But his far legs frolic
Between grassblades, and his tilted ears
Encourage madrigals and hymns
From skylost birds.
His back admires heaven.

As, in a long wind, I would admire him,
Hearing the grass speak,
Enlisting in the blue and dance of birds,
Welcome to eyes that harvest home,
Sharp to glints and goings
Of all this windwhirled.

But am as quiet as a stilled sea,
The almost silent lap, lapse of null
Waves void of hurt, untopped of foam ;
No more than a fallible lisp,
Or a slurring out of a decrepit beard
Of a praise, an unkempt praise
Unheeded in the tall whisper of the grass

Where the birds decline from heaven
In an admiration of decrescent volutes
To fold their songs about him as he goes
In the hope and hurrying of his alation
Among the urge and listen of women,
Loud in the measure of their careful eyes.

I would praise him with my words in the long wind,
With the women and birds and the discrete grassblades.

The birds have sung to him and the grass heard.

AFTER DIVORCE

Caught by the glory of her sensual head,
I forgot for a hectic second that a shade
Should have good manners and not invade
Again her ransomed thoughts or bed.
So I had this unmannerly wish instead
That, if she too had the courtesy to fade
Into the desolation I had made
Out of the sensuality of my head,

I could sleep at last.
                 But at that word,
As at my earlier denials, I heard
My pities and angers under the severe sky
Take once again their destinationless road,
Humbugged and stumbling with their barren load
Of merely obstinate refusals to die.

BIRD ON A JAUNT

Hours ago he woke up the sky,
Has eaten well, now walks about
The kingdom of his confidence,
Feels good, his strong legs
Spur the ground, his neck
Tenses, and he crows again,
A cheer, a challenge,
Just for the hell of it, the gold
Cry vibrant to the horizon,
To the top of the sky, is conscious
Of the sheen of his wings, feels good
This blue morning he has called
Into being, now blesses,
And suddenly purposeful
Strides, prounces, jerks
His mien and mastery
Into the nearest compliant,
Inoffensive brown novice
Of his service, dismounts,
And walks away in the disdain
Of feeling really good this morning.

ADVICE TO A KNIGHT

Wear modest armour ; and walk quietly
In woods, where any noise is treacherous.
Avoid dragons and deceptive maidens.

Be polite to other men in armour,
Especially the fierce ones, who are often strong.
Treat all men as they might be magicians.

So you may come back from your wanderings,
Clink proud and stiff into the queen's court
To doff your helmet and expect her thanks.

The young queen is amused at your white hair,
Asks you to show your notched and rusty sword,
And orders extra straw for your bedding.

Tomorrow put on your oldest clothes,
Take a stout stick and set off again,
It's safer that way if no more rewarding.

WITH HUNGER, WITH ANGER

With hunger, with anger, I shouted for images.
But they eluded me like charities.

There were trees, there were flowers, waiting to be used.
I stumbled on them, remained crazed.

Am still hungry, am still angry, am still
Hunting my forfeit images. I spell

My future, rooting hungrily and angrily
To find an image.
                    Then you show me.

GIRL READING JOHN DONNE

Her arms bare, and her eyes naked,
She tells her borrowed book, *I am in love,*
And the fierce poem jumps about under her skin.

Mr, the almost anonymous lecturer
Who prescribed this text for her undoing,
When he said *Goodmorrow* to his shaving self,
Remembered how she crossed her legs in class,
Thought vaguely of writing a poem, a declaration,
But after breakfast went on marking assignments.

The girl sits blazing in the Library,
Alight over the poem to which she says
I am in love, I am in love. And the poem's
Words flame up to her unseeing eyes.
She does not need to read, only remember
The poem says *I love* to her exposed
And wanted flesh.

                She reads naked in the Library.

Mr every now and again is deflected
From his marking, boredom, marking time,
To wonder momentarily if he was right
To ask of vulnerable innocence
What it thinks about the imprisonment
Of a great Prince.

                His automatic pencil,
Cancelling an ampersand, dismisses
The futile question. He feels morally secure
Because he didn't interrogate them,
Her, about her, his favourite Elegie.
At that minding of bed's America
He resolutely goes on marking.

                It's marking time.

And the naked girl in the Library
Reads a naked poem to herself, and says
I am in love, I am in love, over and over
Until the poem's canicule and sear
Become unbearable, when she burns out
To dissertate over a coke or coffee
On anything, anything except this poem,
This love, bare longing, that bed, this poem.

And elsewhere a great Prince in prison lies.

ADAM AND EVE HEAR THE THUNDER

All their bravado in that grove
Was dissipated like the light,
And their prerogative of love
Was cancelled from the bitter date

When, lying on slack limbs, they heard
About their shamed and burrowing heads,
Not the charmed descant of the bird
Who'd blessed them on their previous beds,

But from the skies reverberate
And make resound the clammy sod
The ineluctable and irate
Brag of the artillery of God.

ADAM WONDERS ABOUT EVE

She writhes so
In her hair's ambiguous clouds
How should I know the truth of this temptation ?

I could believe
Easily she taught the serpent how to speak,
My fluent Eve, nurse of my indecision.

Or did she make
The story up ? invent behind her eyes
The talking snake as one more pet illusion

With which to drown
Me as I drown between her palpable breasts,
Her lord, her clown, twitched at her animation ?

Lord, I eat.
I do not know if eating's right or wrong.
But Lord I eat careless at her instruction.

AGAINST WANTONNESS

Grandfather Adam, who first tried
The use of a divining-rod,
Found such pleasure when Eve cried
He no longer envied God.

So God chastised him in the bushes,
Made it divinely plain,
Though Eve looked charming in her blushes
They must not take such joy again.

But sweat and labour in the night
Only for procreative duty
And not formutual delight.
And kiss therod of sterner beauty.

A WELSH POET FINDS A
PROPER STORY

The story told in the beginning garden
He breathes now, wants to shout it on
His ruined, cuddled paper, crying back
To the longago tree he climbed in Wales,
And asks for pardon.

On this loud paper he says I make that fable,
The woman in the tree, the grounded serpent,
And the treed paper is a white covenant
Damn-Adaming him to be his proper marker,
Initial syllable.

He will be humble to the paper serpent,
Cry down the woman and begin the garden
Over, crossed in an old grave story
A climbed tree told him guilty as promised.
Paper nor words relent.

In a garden beginning he finds a proper story
And lets the paper bellow, bark and build it
For him while he cradles in the treetop in Wales
His silence and the serpent and the woman
And all that glory.

IV.

THE COLOUR OF COCKCROWING
(*for Robyn*)

It was always the colour of cockcrowing. On the first morning
Of creation Leviathan lifted his mighty shoulders
Above the waves and saw the colour of the cockcrow.
And on the following mornings, bull, and stallion,
Roebuck, reindeer, rhinoceros, the timid mouse,
The moose, eland, okapi, kangaroo, jerboa,
Fox, badger, otter, seal, and all the birds,
Sun-daring eagle, vulture already aware of death,
The great sea-spanning albatross, swallow,
Lark, and nightingale, the murderous Christmas robin,
Brawling sparrow, and laughing kookaburra,
And the fish, the sainted herring, and the holy salmon,
Mackerel, bream, and bass, sardine, and shark,
Perch, pilchard, trout, and coelacanth,
Insects, flies, spiders, bees, wasps, hornets, locusts,
Reptiles, giant boas and the deadly mambas,
Great king cobras and black Papuan snakes,
Crocodiles, alligators, duck-billed platypi,
The natives and anomalies of the world,
They all looked out on their first morning
And knew at once the colour of cockcrowing.

And God made Adam, and after Adam, Eve.
And Adam knew, even as he delighted
In the world about him, the colour of cockcrowing.
And Eve knew too, and when she took the apple,
Gave it to Adam that they might share their knowledge.

The cock crew first when those two put on leaves.
The cock has crown in your hearts and in mine
Since Adam hid himself among the trees,
And Eve lay waiting for him somewhere.

Crow, cock, until this woman and this man
Return to dust, crow until their children
And their children's children too are dust,
Crow until God revoke his first decree
That Earth and all the inhabitants thereof
Should wear forever the colour of cockcrowing.

In the world we know it was always the colour of the cockcrow.

UNCOLLECTED POEMS

NOT WHEN I CAME

Not when I came
With anger and tall drum
Ranger of seas
To pull down towns
Ravener of forests
Uprooter of mountains
Not when I came
Tall in my danger
Did your proud refuge
Fall to my storm.

But when at nightfall
Weary with wounds
Slashed drum trailing
War-cry silent
I sat down to weep
You opened your gates
To let me conquer
Your proud refusal.

THINKING TO WRITE AN ODE

Thinking to write an ode, to avoid elegy,
And to exceed for once the lyric impulse
As brief and long-lasting as last night's love-making,
To avoid also satire and the desire to tell
You what you already ought to know—
Thinking to write an ode, I thought of my country
Which has been for centuries an elegy,
And where everybody speaks always in lyrics,
And you have to be satirical to keep sane
As we tell each other what we already know—
And then, thinking to write an ode, I thought of love,
And of how the best of love is always somehow elegiac,
Though also brittle and enduring as lyrics,
And in defence against love we resort to satire,
And tell ourselves what we already know.

Thinking to write an ode, I thought of these things,
And thought—are odes impossible in these bloody days?
And told myself what I already know.

LOST LOVE, UNWRITTEN POEMS

Once I would have fretted, been ill at ease
To think that now your love and loving body
Of old devoted so tenderly to me
Were now another's to do with as he please.

Once I would have fretted in weak discontent
Before the blank despairing of a page
I'd sit and look at or scribble on an age
Unable to write the poem that I meant.

But, praise be, the withering into age
Brings some small mercies, and among them this :
Now an unwritten poem or unkissed kiss
Can stir no more to any sort of rage.

Once I would have fretted and soaked my brow
With sweat over such things.
                                        As I do now.

P IS FOR POETRY

Predicaments of landscape, old despairs,
Roads not taken on for wrong reasons,
And the importunate belly of the sea
—Should these invoke a proper catalogue
Of your and mine lost and invented seasons ?

Paradox of language or of love,
What speech had I before you gave me tongue ?
Before that and before that was the sea.
The sea gave birth to you, and something else
Spoke from the waters before I was young.

Paragraphs of landscape, seascape, now
Elude me more than any original love.
Ghosts of my guesses flaunt and parade
Where once the possibility of the word
Lurked around, about, and treacherously above.

Paragraphs, paradox, predicaments
—But how should my inadequate language make
Even from landscapes or from love
The one poem to show poems unnecessary
—And that it was for your dear, sea-born sake ?

THEY LIE
(*for Madeleine*)

They lie, who tell me love is such
That nothing else would matter
If I could only touch
Her once and love her ever after.
They lie.

They lie, who tell me love is such
It's no more than a matter
Of near enough to touch
Her rightly and then leave her after.
They lie.

They lie—and yet our love is such
That it seems to matter.
And if we do not touch, or if we touch,
Whatever they say after,
They lie.

ARE THERE ANY MODERN POETS

(for Madeleine)

Mimic, you called me, and said I had that comic
Gift, and I was pleased with what I took to be
A compliment, and all the while my heart—
Romantic property—was ill at ease
Feeling that it belonged to a tragic hero,
Doomed to a doomed love,—and so I said
"Heart, stop beating ; a modern poet
Doesn't write that sort of poetry"—and my heart
Told me that I am an old-fashioned poet
Writing over and over again, My love.

LOVE, POETRY, AND MIDDLE AGE

Poets have written much about love's madness,
And much of this was mere convention, granted,
But still convention can embody truth,
And what sane man has ever wanted
His age to duplicate the joy and sadness
Love brought him in his youth ?

But it happens, and it's not much use to blame
The poets—some of them have suffered too.
All this I tell you in an offhand way.
Perhaps it's lust, I add—then you :
"I am indifferent to the choice of name ;
I'm glad you're here today."

RESTLESS

Restless, I rose
And walked out at some shivery hour
After midnight, hoping to exorcize
Whatever it was that would not let me sleep.

The silent streets, the sleeping houses,
Soothed me, and the distant sea.

Then insolently from behind a cloud
The moon appeared.
                              Helpless, I turned
Back to my restless bed, knowing
That while you rule me and I wait
For your inevitable stroke
I cannot even hope to wish for peace.

NO NAME BUT LOVE

And you invite me to your bed.
How should I react ? With terror,
Delight, mere animal expectancy ?
—No, none of these, or all of these,
Adding up in love's arithmetic
To something more than all of these,
Something for which we have no name but love.

A SORT OF LOVE POEM

Boasting merely of the bodily contact
He made the thump and slump of his body seem
An incorrigible animal act
Which never really measured to his dream.

This other, boasting of finer attitudes,
The delicate way he had of cherishing,
Made women only mirrors of his moods,
While for the act itself he was not perishing.

I would be neither of these men—I mean
I would be both of them : give you my body
Willingly when you choose, or wean
Me when you like to love you abstractly.

But let me boast in either case, that I
Loved you too much to boast of loving you.
Bodies or not, I only want to lie
And do whatever it is you want to do.

ADAM, THOUGHTFULLY, TO EVE

Half awake, I heard you murmur to my side,
And half awake I turned to you, and then
All the great trumpets sounded, and you sighed
Your dear command to do the deed again.
And if my upright passion had not died
In you, how could there have been other men
For other women to turn to half awake
To love them so, as I do for your sake ?

FIREWORKS NIGHT

A rocket soars, explodes, and dies away,
And I turn helplessly to you to say
Something, as usual inadequate,
And, as usual too, I am too late,
For you are watching in the bonfire's glow
Somebody else who might have loved you so.

URGENCY

Urgency was what I always felt with you,
The importunate need of being closer together,
The impossible demand to defeat mere
Momentariness, to enjoy for ever
The pulsing richness of your summer season.
Even my ghost will go urgently
Across the pallid pastures to meet your ghost,
And in an echo trembling with impatience
Make again impossible demands, urging
That love be not a matter of seasons, nor
Subject to limits, especially then,
Bound to our incorporeality.

IN THIS DEGENERATE AGE

To have this at least in common with Solomon :
Not wisdom certainly, but to be prone
To this disturbance when a virgin,
Probable or improbable, sidles
That look at my hoary and distinguished
Hairs.
            But times have changed. No doubt
We are less mighty men now in the bed.
A mere half-dozen women last any of us moderns
More than a lifetime.
                        I console myself
That even Solomon had but the one Sheba,
And in that at least I do as well as he did.

VERBALIST

It is the verbalist in me concedes
That love is not to be destroyed by words
Despite the impediments that we admit,
Being not so single-purposed as those birds
That mate in the blue emptiness of air.
Lacking in pride, we must make do with wit
To salvage from the bedwreck of our deeds
Whatever unity we hope to share
From this compounding of passion and despair.

Let me then remain part verbalist
At least, if only enough to indicate
To interested parties that we would not love
At any lesser or less dangerous rate,
Our virtue being in our infirmity.
We may not couple in that heaven above,
We may not have there for antagonist
These words which lend a little dignity
To our bedreckoned, bedfound duality.

Nor would there seem to be necessity
To keep the verbalist in me apart
From the swaggering funambulist
Swaying above the plaudits of your heart
And only sorry when the act is done.
You did not ask for words when first we kissed
Though since you've had some superfluity.
Our war of words and love is lost and won
In the same bed where it has just begun.

THE GOLD CLARITY OF THIS MOMENT

Observe the gold clarity of this moment,
And ask, inveterate questioner, how much
Of this is sheerly there, how much is
The impact of the external on five
Uncertain receptors—is that colour there,
That gold invitation of her hair ?
Or the astonishing blue welcome of her eyes ?
This tenderness I touch, does it exist ?
Or those low sounds I hear, this heady
Inhalation, or this tang I taste ?

Ask in the gold clarity of this moment
—If you dare—how far these things exist,
How far they are created—if that's the word—
By your own impossible longing.

Epistemology was never my strong point.
Observing the gold clarity of this moment
I know there is only one way in which I want
To know you and know we know each other.

FROM WHENCE COMETH MY HELP

Cloudburst, sunblast, tiderip, bedwrack,
I knew on holy hills, long, long ago.
If I had known then what now I unholily know,
Would I have followed the worm and sheepdropped track
To which I now nostalgically look back
As once in deserts I was starved for snow ?
Or would I still say to that lumper, Go,
Boy, out, and down, so, possibly, back ?

Improper question. I am what I may be.
I went, out, and down, and here, at last,
To suffer, suffer, over and over again,
That hillborn appetency for pain,
Tiderip, bedwrack, cloudburst, sunblast,
And whatever else is mine ineluctably.

STORMS ETC.

Storms I had been through before, heaved
My heart up into the sick and towering green ;
And storms I could survive, however obscene
The way in which I grieve for them, and through them grieved.

Storms are one thing, but this is not a storm :
Merely your incredible cool saying
That you no longer feel the need for weighing
How much I am now worth your keeping warm.

The only answer to a tempest is a kiss :
But how can I, creeping into middle age,
Evoke the proper and very loving rage
To say, Leave if you must, but not like this ?

Come, darling, make me sick again in storms ;
At least permit the grapple of my hands
To show you once more where your true love stands
As witness how your blood his blood still warms.

And then I can face any storm again,
Blinded with your spindrift, sick, heartsick,
But with the knowledge quickening in my quick
We share each other in our separate pain.

NEVER AN ARMISTICE

Now in midwinter and still at war :
Though frozen into attrition, we are numbly
Waiting for the cruel coming of flowers
And the hurt of sap beginning to move
To announce to us that we are again free
To grapple each other's bodies, die once more
Upon each other still more bloodily.
Not even midwinter brings us peace, only
This temporary lull and preparation
For renewal of combat to perpetuity
—Never an armistice between you and me.

MEMORIES OF A COUNTRY CHILDHOOD

The bull upon the cow : in those rough days
I had not heard of Pasiphae, nor dreamed
Of you for mounting as I must do now.

The nervous horse urgent upon the mare
Would be a better image of what I feel
When I dream of burning Troy for your bright hair.

The boar grunting upon the sow not that,
My sensibility's appalled even as I grunt
And grant you what we've both been aiming at.

The other animals deserted Paradise :
We were expelled, but in each other's eyes
We saw the better promise of this one rise :
Man has the luck that more than once he dies

THE HUNGER OF THIS LOVE

The hunger of this love
Picks on its own bonefeast,
Wanting the one guest
To spill the wedding salt,
Asperge this married guilt,
Return this love.

Your unborn children cry
That I have been afraid ;
Words that I have said
Wound my intending mouth
As my wishes gutter forth
To you, today.

Banquet me not, nor give
Me supper to assuage
This want with which I rage.
Bring only bread and wine
So, when at last we dine,
You give, forgive.

THE PENDULUM

What will come
Quick to the window
Where I lie
Beneath the tall
Tick-tock, tick-tock
Of the ready clock ?
What will come
To tell me I die ?

What will come,
Angel or troll,
To catch and stop
The pendulum
And my quick,
Angel or troll
To lift me to the sky
Or let me drop
To that old hell ?
Troll or angel,
What will come ?

What will come ?
I see its shadow
Lean on the sill
But cannot tell
If it be angel
Or sulky troll.
The shadow stays
A hand licks out

I hear the last
Tick-tock, tick-tock
Of quick and clock.
The pendulum
Is caught, is caught,
And what has come ?

THE GREEN TREE

Caught young, I grew to be a pretty boy,
Fondled and dandled on many a lovely lap,
Called precious and a pet as well as pretty,
But the green tree keeps on growing,
Those ladies did not tell me of old age,
Of how reticulate wrinkles would creep
To cover their faces, lips grow dry
While the green tree keeps on growing.

Lissom ladies who were fond of me
I praise your unstrained quality of kindness
And all your wanton and your merry ways
While the green tree kept on growing.
Now that your limbs are grown rheumatic
Look at me out of your vague and clouded eyes
And assert I was indeed a pretty boy
But the green tree kept on growing.

LOVE'S OVERTONES

It is a terrible thing to be young, young
With that vitality unaware
Of the secure depredations of age. Only
The old know the civility of death.

We are all subjects of sea-change, and change.
Tall colums lie and crumble in undergrowth.
Imperial bones moulder as surely
As your beautiful ones or the always rotten.

It is a terrible thing to be young, but more
Terrible to be aware of growing old
Simultaneously with the shock of you,
Your ignorant hair clouding the calm sky.

A conscious terror, therefore more terrible.
Meanwhile I keep my shudder in my bones,
And look at you in lust and wonderment.
Terror and death are but love's overtones.

USELESS ADVICE TO A YOUNG MAN
HOPELESSLY IN LOVE

If not of this, then of some other despair
Grow fat and sleek. Be sure there are enough.
I made a memorandum once of hair
And filed it irrevocably somewhere.

Seek not green pastures, be content with stone.
Their virtue is they cannot make you sick.
And meditate once daily on the bone :
It's almost permanent, and it's your own.

Do not expect even wise men to be wise.
Wisdom, at best, is incommunicable.
Look greedily into her greedy eyes,
And try to tell only convincing lies.

Put not your trust in words or anything.
Put not your trust in really saying enough.
Birds in the hand can't be compelled to sing.
Despair suffices. Love's something else . . . something.

PASTORAL

An old ram, slithering along the fog,
Obeying a familiar, difficult command,
See, how he snuffles now and comes to stand
For what they used to importunately beg.

He is too old. As he lets his shrunken knees
Sink regretfully to earth again, his ewes
Maternally gossip of how he would use
Them in the old days, how he could please.

Young rams horn in ; and old rams must retreat.
Young ewes become old ewes in one sharp spring
(Young lambs they tell us make the sweetest meat.)
This old ram, had they done this one swift thing
To him, would not now need to grudge the young
Rams mount the ewes he once was lord among.

HEART, MIND, AND BODY

HEART

Patience, you counselled : when you look for it least
That love will come to take you unawares
So that you know then you have known it always.

MIND

Was I not right to counsel thus ? Did not
Love come and take you unawares
So that you know now you have known him always ?

BODY

You never counselled me that love would come
Repeatedly to take me unawares
Though what I knew cannot be known for always.

I let you hear this internecine
Conversation so that you know that for you only
I am this unequal triumvirate,
Aware now that I am yours for always.

BUT THAT WAS IN
ANOTHER COUNTRY

Love, that old, notorious country
I have wandered far from,
Said the old beachcomber,
Is still, you know, a proper land
Where such as you and I may learn
Between the downing of the sun
And its uprising
What the bloody world is for.

Love, that new and fabulous country
I am pressing on for,
Said the brash explorer,
Is bound to be, you know, a land
Where such as you and I may learn
Between the rising of the sun
And (I'm afraid) its downing
What this brightest world is for.

Love, that oldest, newest country
I have said so much about,
Said the young grandfather,
Is, I suppose, a bounden land
Where such as you and I must learn
Between the downing of one sun
And the downing of another
What these women want us for.

NOT ON THIS CONTINENT

It is no good : not on this continent
Shall I get rid of my chains
Said the old poet
And the old convict agreed.

I thought here, now,
Said the old poet
To get rid of my chains :
There's no hope, son, said the old convict.

But you don't wear yours any more,
The poet said to the convict,
And the convict said to the poet,
You haven't noticed the way I walk.

And the convict said to the poet,
You never had any chains, son.
And the poet replied,
You haven't noticed the way I write.

And they both agreed
It isn't any good on this continent
And decided over a beer
To emigrate to Australia or somewhere

INDEX TO TITLES

INDEX TO FIRST LINES

263

265

81
22-45